GARY PLAYER

In recent times, only four men have won
the 'Grand Slam' of golf — the U.S. Open,
British Open, the Masters and the
U.S.P.G.A. title. One of these four is
Gary Player.

This feat has been achieved by
determination and hard work, both on
and off the golf course. Player believes
that physical and mental conditioning
have a major role in playing *positive golf*.

In this book he has set down his rules
for conditioning himself in a clear readable
style. He gives tips on how to think on a
golf course as well as how to practise and
how to play. POSITIVE GOLF is one of
the most stimulating and valuable books
of golf instruction ever published.

Gary Player's

Positive Golf

Understanding and Applying
the Fundamentals of the Game

CORGI BOOKS
TRANSWORLD PUBLISHERS LTD
A National General Company

POSITIVE GOLF

A CORGI BOOK 552 08383 6

Originally published in Great Britain
by Cassell & Co. Ltd.

PRINTING HISTORY

Cassell Edition published 1967
Corgi Edition published 1970

Copyright © 1967 by Golf Marks N.V.

This book is set in 11 on 12 pt Times 327

Corgi Books are published by Transworld Publishers Ltd.,
Bashley Road, London, N.W. 10.

Made and printed in Great Britain by
Fletcher & Son Ltd., Norwich, Norfolk.

PREFACE

My first contact—literally—with golf was through my toes! My boyhood friends and I haunted the water hazards of a golf course near my Johannesburg, South Africa, home. We'd wade out and, with only our heads sticking up above the water, use our toes to feel for golf balls in the mud.

My first "clubs" were only sticks with a piece of wire bent into a "clubhead." When we were tired of soccer, cricket, track, and swimming, we'd chop at those water-logged balls with our makeshift clubs.

Golf was strictly a minor sport to me when I was fourteen, and I was surprised one day when my father, a middle-handicap player, invited me to a round at the Virginia Park course.

My first game was a revelation. Tagging along with Father and three of his friends, I actually parred the first three holes! They weren't difficult holes, but pars are pars. Later, of course, I made plenty of sixes and sevens, but I enjoyed myself thoroughly and soon golf became my main interest.

It was at Virginia Park that I first met Vivienne Verwey, daughter of Jack Verwey, the golf professional there. I went into the pro shop to get some tees during that first year of golf and there she was, lovely in a pink sweater, behind the counter. Soon I was joining Viv and her brother Bobby, now a tournament professional himself, in golf nearly every weekend. We put up 2 shillings each, about 24 cents, for the first to break 50. I did so when I was fifteen, and it was a great thrill.

Viv herself became a fine two-handicap golfer, and might have developed into one of the world's better lady competitors had she not married me. Once, after we were married and I had turned professional, we played a friendly match. I offered her strokes, but she would have none of this, and she beat my 71! Since then, Jennifer, Mark, Wayne, Michele, and Theresa have come along, and I no longer have to worry about fairway competition from Viv!

When I first set out to become a golf champion, only a few people—probably only my father and my wife—believed I would make it. I'll be ever thankful for their faith and patience during my apprenticeship. I could never have gone as far as I have without their encouragement, and therefore I would like to dedicate this book to them.

I would also like to thank my friend Dick Aultman and his staff at *Golf Digest* magazine for their fine help in preparing the chapters that follow.

CONTENTS

Gary Player's

Positive Golf

1
LESSONS I'VE LEARNED

From the time I was very young, I realized how hard my father worked for a living in the gold mines, drilling all day long 10,000 feet underground. Because of his example, I grew up knowing you cannot be a success in life if you don't work hard.

This lesson certainly applies in golf. I came into my chosen profession realizing the value of a stroke. I did not want to waste a single swing, knowing that one shot might make my future or break it. This is a very important attitude, one that all the truly great players possess. They couldn't be great if they didn't have it.

Lesser golfers never learn the full value of a stroke. I believe you only learn it by working hard and appreciating the value of hard work. There are a lot of fellows who have been given everything all their lives . . . or perhaps they have the gift of too much natural ability.

"What the hell, what's a shot?" you hear them say. They are mistaken—each shot is important.

This is why I've always been extremely conscientious—almost a fanatic—about practicing. Some people say that, except for maybe Ben Hogan, I've practiced longer and harder than any other golfer today. I think they are probably right.

As a boy growing up in Johannesburg, I remember practicing about as hard as a human being could. Playing truant from school, I would go out with my clubs in the morning and hit balls all day long until six in the evening—with only an hour for lunch and maybe a half-hour nap on days when it was very warm. The whole day was golf.

I practiced my wedge to start with, hitting a bag of balls into the sand trap. Then I'd go into the bunker and hit the balls out onto the green. I wouldn't leave that bunker until I'd holed five shots. I'd just stay there until I'd done it, even if it took two or three hours.

After the sand shots I'd practice something else, perhaps chipping. Here, too, I had my own private self-imposed goal; I had to chip ten into the hole before I'd quit.

In those days, I carried my own flag. Sticking it into the fairway, I'd hit a bunch of 7-irons to it. Then I'd go on to all the other clubs and, finally, back to putting.

Always when putting, I'd imagine I was about to win one of the major tournaments, saying to myself, "This one's for the U.S. Open, Gary . . . the British Open," and so forth. It was a long hard day for a youngster, but I never grew tired of going out to the course. I believed then—and still do—that your wildest dreams come true.

But I knew if I were ever to become a champion professional golfer I would have to work at it, and work at it harder than the next man, for my size and weight were both against me.

To build up my legs, I ran. My older brother Ian always went with me, up and down the dusty gold-mine hills. When I wanted to quit after running only a mile or so, he wouldn't let me. Because of Ian I came to realize that I *could* keep going when I thought I couldn't. Over the years, I've made a lot of money in golf by not giving up when the going got rough and it looked as if there weren't a chance. I'd rather finish fortieth than fiftieth; I'd rather win $100 than $10. There are a lot of guys who say, "If I can't win the tournament or finish in the first ten I don't care if I'm out of the money." Not so with me.

To build up my arms, I did push-ups—with Ian standing over me counting, not letting me quit. In those days I did seventy fingertip push-ups, spread throughout a day, trying to build up my thin arms.

Yet, with all this regular exercise—attempting to compensate for my 5-foot-7-inch stature—I still found myself playing a practice round at the Masters in 1960 and unable to reach the par-5's on my second shot. All the top players were knocking it onto the par-5 greens in two, but I couldn't.

I spoke to Peter Thomson about it and he said he didn't think he could ever win the Masters because he was such a short hitter. He just couldn't get it to the green on the par-5's either—I decided right then and there to do something about my problem.

I began working with professional body-builders—

3

(1) Successful tournament professionals have an opportunity to delve into many business ventures. My off-course activity is handled by Mark McCormack, shown with me, a fine friend who is very good at his job.

(2) Five of my leading fans follow me and my caddie, David McIntyre, in the 1966 British Open. They are Michele, then 2; Wayne, 5; Mark, 6; Jennifer, 8, and my wife, Vivienne. Our baby, Theresa, will be making it a sixsome soon, I'm sure.

(3) Children, I believe, are among some of my best fans on the U.S. tournament circuit. Here something I said draws laughter and some big smiles—except for that tow-headed sobersides on the left.

(4) Here I study a new golf-bag design with Michael Davis, with whose golf-accessory manufacturing firm I am associated.

(5) Sometimes I find it helpful to study other players' styles. Here I'm taking some movies of a professional. Later on, I studied the films at my leisure.

(6) Perseverance will pay off in golf. Once I practiced sand trap shots until I could hole out five shots. As a result, today I am confident of putting the ball at least close to the cup from the sand.

4

5

even hired a trainer for a while—concentrating on the push-ups and knee bends, skipping rope and working out with the weights and other exercises.

A year later, in 1961, I won the Masters. That year a national magazine ran a survey on just where drives had landed. Figures showed my tee shots had landed very close to Arnold Palmer's! And at Augusta in 1965 I had the best score of the field on the par-5's— even beating the winner, Jack Nicklaus, by one stroke on these holes that once had been too long for me. I feel I owe this added distance mostly to those body-building exercises.

Although the exercises have been very important to my game, so is the fact that in my early days as a professional in South Africa I gave literally hundreds —maybe thousands—of golf lessons. Teaching forces you to analyze your own techniques, to come to grips with the fundamentals of the game, which means you're in an excellent position to uncover and solve the problem when some part of your game goes sour.

This fundamental knowledge of the golf swing is very important for any golfer who hopes to succeed, but it is vital for players who earn their living by playing the game. There are some members of the professional tour—Jack Nicklaus comes quickly to my mind—who have this knowledge. When their games go sour, they can quickly discover and correct the fundamental problems. Yet, many others on the tour—even some of the better players—lack a sound basic knowledge of the golf swing. When these players encounter trouble, it may take them months —even years—to recover their form.

If there's one thing I've learned, it's to play golf your own way, instead of playing like somebody else.

But you still have to know the fundamentals. And you still have to try to adjust your game to the facts of life when you're a small man like myself. When you're being outdriven by these big men by 20 or 30 yards, you must adjust yourself not to let that worry you, to continue to play your own game—making sure to get in some good putts. Putting, as they say, makes up for a lot of yardage—putting and a good basic understanding of the fundamentals.

If you ask a lot of fairly good golfers what they are thinking about when they hit the ball, they'll say, "Nothing. I just hit it." This isn't right. You must know exactly *what* you are doing, *why* it results in a good shot, *how* it's happening. Otherwise it's just luck, and there'll come a day when you can no longer reproduce your results, a day when you won't know why, much less how, to unravel that particular snarl.

The truth is that nobody has enough *natural* ability to become a real champion. You've got to know the fundamentals of the game to get up there and stay up there. You can't ever let yourself become bloody well self-satisfied with your game. Developing your game —whether you are a Sunday golfer or a pro on the tour—is a process of continual correction and, I feel, the development of a sound, sustained program of physical conditioning.

In short, I feel that to play golf to the best of your ability you should (1) understand the fundamentals of the game and (2) prepare yourself physically and mentally. In the instruction chapters that follow I will explain these fundamentals and tell how to condition yourself so that you can execute them properly.

2

CONDITIONING YOURSELF
FOR BETTER GOLF

Without the emphasis I placed on building and maintaining this 153-pound body of mine, I simply wouldn't be where I am today, successfully competing against usually bigger golfers, many of whom tower over me by 6 inches and outweigh me by 50 pounds.

I only wish I could write now how it actually feels to work out. Once you begin exercising religiously, it's the greatest sensation in the world—soon you feel you *have* to work out. It becomes an addiction, but it's a habit that pays dividends for a professional golfer or a weekend player trying to cut a few strokes from his game.

Strangely enough, it seems that precious few golfers believe in exercising. When it comes to keeping our bodies in good working condition, we golfers are probably the laziest lot of athletes on earth. All

Golf muscles may be strengthened by swinging the iron bar from a set of bar bells.

around the world football players, trackmen, and swimmers all work out with weights ·and perform calisthenics. But not golfers. By and large, with a few outstanding exceptions, golfers couldn't care less about their bodies. I guess they just don't realize that muscles can make such a vast difference in their games.

Being in good physical shape has meant the big difference for me on many an afternoon. For instance, when I get in deep rough, instead of taking an 8-iron and playing short of the green, I can swing a 6-iron through the heavy grass and hit all the way to the hole.

But you needn't take my word. For living, breathing proof that extra strength and good muscle tone influence your game, you only have to look at today's best tournament professionals. To a man, they are powerful, capable of hitting great distances and, perhaps more important, fighting their way out of trouble spots through sheer strength. Everyone has noticed how well Billy Casper has played since he has lost weight. Jack Nicklaus and Arnold Palmer can thank their muscles for a great deal of their success.

Since a very early age, I have been what you might call a nut about physical conditioning. The importance of this first struck home when I was attending King Edward College (similar to a U.S. high school) in Johannesburg. Although I was smaller than most of my teammates, I was a varsity performer in both cricket and rugby. I was honored by being elected captain for both teams in my senior year.

However, it is only in recent years that I began to study seriously the art of exercise. Not being able to reach those par-5's at the Masters is what told me I needed a better body. So I hired Roy Hilligenn as my physical-fitness instructor—he formerly held the Mr. America and Mr. Universe titles. About this same time, I also began reading a little book that has caused quite a change in my whole outlook on life in many important ways. It's called *Yoga and Health*.

Now, of course, there are many golfers who wouldn't bother to stand on their heads, because it's not quite chic, not in style. I suppose they're afraid of being laughed at. That's understandable. But to tell the truth, I'm just as happy my opponents on the pro circuit haven't investigated the teachings of yoga and the art of exercise. Because if they did, I know they could improve their scores by at least a couple of strokes—strokes that might beat me!

While I'm not what you would call a genuine yoga expert, I've researched it enough to know something about it. Yoga exercises are designed to improve your blood circulation, which in turn helps your body perform to its top capabilities.

Standing on your head encourages good blood circulation through your brain. You'll think more clearly after a short session. If you have been plagued with headaches, this would help.

Tournament golfers often develop backaches. I can relieve this by lying on my back with my heels to-gether, and doing a reverse arch. A good yoga neck exercise is to lie on your back with your feet off the ground, holding them there as long as you can.

The thing about yoga exercises—as well as the more conventional workouts—is the way they *give* you energy rather than take it away from you. Often

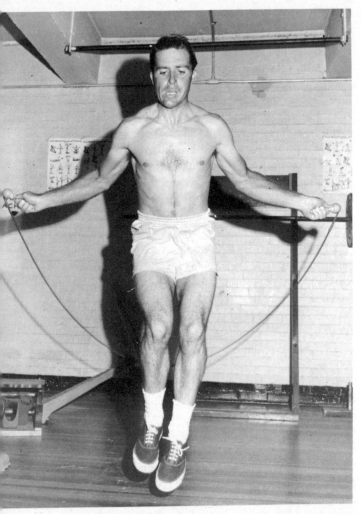

Skipping rope will improve your swing by developing rhythm and faster hand and leg movement.

I begin my exercises feeling absolutely down and out, but by the time I'm finished I feel great again.

I've found that the particular exercises we golfers need most are those that develop our hands and our lower arms, our lower back muscles, and, of course, our legs. You should be very careful, however, not to do too much body conditioning that might over-develop your neck, shoulders, chest, and upper-arm muscles. Overdeveloping these particular muscles isn't good for your golf game. When you have big upper-arm, neck, and chest muscles, you simply can't wind up and unwind freely and easily. It's as simple as that.

Running is probably the best single exercise there is. Plenty of oxygen gets into your blood, improving your circulation and building up your heart muscles. Lately, though, I've done less running. Instead, I do a lot of rope-skipping. I've found skipping's a great way to improve my timing, rhythm, and coordination and to loosen my whole body. More important, skipping rope develops speed in your legs and hands, something every golfer should seek. This becomes especially important as we get older.

I do my exercise routine year round, three times a week, even though all the exercise experts tell me I shouldn't work out during a tournament. Ideally, the best time to do exercises is about two or three o'clock in the afternoon. That's when your body is loosened up, when you're at your strongest. Since I'm usually on the course at that time, I find I'm holding most of my workouts in the evening.

For the best physical condition, systematic exercising should be combined with a sensible diet. Heavy golfers seldom prosper. You're going to get a much better windup and a much better follow-through when you're not overweight. So the kinds of food you eat, and the amount, are extremely important. I believe golfers should concentrate on eating natural types of food, such as steak—Americans have the best beef in the world—and salads and plenty of fresh fruit and fruit juices.

A man who once worked in a health center gave me this breakfast, and I've found it to be great: I start off with a glass of fresh orange juice and half a slice of melon. Then comes the main course: a mixture of nuts, raisins, whole wheat germ, yogurt, sliced bananas, more orange juice, and some raw oats, all combined together like a bowl of cereal.

During golf competition, I'll often have something like this for lunch: a grated apple, a salad, a small piece of meat (not fried), and a glass of milk. Enough to satisfy my hunger but not so much as to make me sluggish. It's never advisable to eat heavily just before you play golf.

For dinner, I'll often have soup, broiled fish, grilled brown toast with honey, and vegetables and fruits. Of course, I vary my meals, but as a rule I'll stick with natural foods and rule out those that have been "refined." I try to stay away from fried cooking, coffee, tea, white sugar, and white breads. In making white bread, for instance, all the wheat germ is sifted out and only what is left is used. For those of you who hope to lose some weight, I suggest strongly that you cut out all white foods—white sugar, potatoes, white bread, and dairy products. You'll find you will lose weight very quickly. I know this is what many of the touring professionals are doing now.

I find that for me and my game, careful eating

habits go hand in hand with good sleeping habits. Some people feel they can get along with only six hours of sleep. Others need ten. I need a minimum of nine. Find out what's best for you and stick to a schedule.

Being in good shape also offers other dividends to a golfer, whether he's traveling a quarter-million miles a year as I do or not. I'm referring to the business of having your game go stale. It isn't the constant playing under tension or the practicing that causes golfers to lose their edge. Rather, the fault more often lies with the fact that you've let your body run down because of lack of exercise, sleep, and proper eating habits. In good physical condition, a body easily absorbs the punishment of playing under constant tension for those long hours, even on an empty stomach. The next few months could make all the difference in your game. By following a carefully thought-out routine of sleeping, eating, and exercising, you can soon work yourself into top shape, whatever your age, and I'll guarantee you'll be shooting better golf.

A SYSTEMATIC PROGRAM FOR DEVELOPING YOUR GOLF MUSCLES

This exercise program is designed especially for golfers. I follow it myself. I feel that this program not only develops the muscles you need for golf, but that it also will help you enjoy your everyday living more fully. These exercises will actually develop muscle bulk as well as muscle tone and stamina. The equipment you will need to perform these exercises is

EXERCISE 1: With elbows at your side, rotate dumbbells to outside, then to inside. This builds hand, wrist, and forearm muscles.

EXERCISE 2: With forearms resting on thighs, raise and lower weight—first with hands above bar, then under bar. Good for forearms.

EXERCISE 3: Holding a small weight on the back of your neck, rotate shoulders so elbows touch thighs. This strengthens the back muscles.

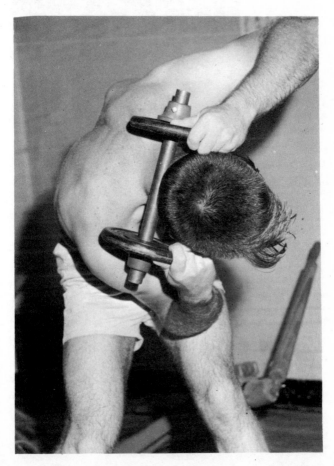

EXERCISE 4: With weight across the back of the neck, bend forward and then return to upright position. This builds strength in the lower back.

EXERCISE 5: Turning with weight behind back in simulated golf swing will improve your body turn.

EXERCISE 6: With weight across shoulders, do a series of half-squats. This will increase bulk and strength of thighs.

EXERCISE 7: Again with weight across the back, do a series of toe-rises. This strengthens the calves for improved footwork.

available at most gymnasiums, or can be purchased for just a few dollars.

Naturally, the extent of exercise and the amount of weight one can handle at first will vary with the individual. Therefore, I advise that you consult an experienced weight-lifter or physical-education expert before starting your program. Also, I advise against daily workouts. Allow yourself a day of rest between each session. And finally, never lift weights before your body is warm and your muscles are loose. A session of skipping rope should precede every workout.

3

THINK YOUR WAY TO LOWER SCORES

A strange thing happened to me before the 1965 U.S. Open at Bellerive Country Club near St. Louis. I was walking past the master scoreboard, which includes the names, lettered in gold, of all previous Open winners. Ken Venturi's name was last on the list as 1964 winner. Just below it was lettered the current year—*1965*—with space alongside for that year's winner.

Then, suddenly, I saw it—my name lettered in that space. I really saw it! It was bright gold just like the others: G-A-R-Y P-L-A-Y-E-R.

All during the Open I visualized myself winning, and going up to receive the trophy. I imagined how I would accept the trophy, how I would hold it, what I would say. I even saw how I would play the last hole, needing a four to win. And all that I had foreseen came true. I even needed a four to tie Kel Nagle and force the play-off.

Concentrating in golf must last until the very end. Here I
check my scorecard carefully after winning the 1965 U.S.
Open in a play-off with Kel Nagle.

This experience at the Open was strange, but an-
ticipating is part of my mental makeup in golf. I've
conditioned myself, for instance, to visualize the
path of my shots before I play them. I always believe
in positive thinking. To me, it's all part of concentration.

What you think while playing golf is probably the
most important single part of your game. It's surprising how many golfers hit the ball well but still fail to
become really good golfers. They have great swings

and wallop the ball a long way, but they don't play winning golf.

Equally surprising are those who start golf with almost no promise of ability whatsoever but have improved each time you see them—and continue to improve. The difference between an ordinary player and a champion is the way they think.

It's as simple as this: If you don't concentrate, you're not playing your best. There's absolutely no question that golf is a game of mind over matter. There come those rare occasions when a player's mental and physical makeups are in such a high degree of tune that he finds it possible to direct his muscles to pull off shots he'd normally consider impossible; days when he *knows* the putts are going to drop. This holds true whether you're playing the tour or doing most of your golfing only on Saturdays and Sundays. A golfer has to discipline his mind to keep absolute attention on what's happening that very moment—not on the bogey he made on the last hole or on the tough par-5 coming up next, but on the particular shot at hand to the exclusion of everything else.

Concentration takes years of practice to acquire. It's difficult to come by, and easy to lose if you let up. An integral part of developing concentration, of course, is self-discipline—the kind of self-control that teaches your mind to do what you want it to do.

The ways I practice self-discipline include going without the ice cream I really want; forcing myself sleepily out of bed at the same time each morning; never postponing my exercises. These methods help me develop the self-control that is so important out on the course during a tense tournament.

Yoga is also a method I use for increasing my powers of concentration and self-control. Some of the ideas of yoga help a golfer focus and concentrate his attention on a single problem. (In Chapter 2 I mentioned some of the yoga exercises I do.)

I never knew how to relax when I was a young boy, and I still find it hard to unwind completely. But yoga has enabled me to relax, especially during tournament play. For example, during every major championship I've won I concentrated so hard that I played rounds without knowing my score! I've often been in a don't-know-who-I-am sort of daze—total relaxation with complete control.

Many golfers have nothing wrong with their games. They simply lack confidence. I hear many men feeling sorry for themselves, dropping comments such as "Gee, I'm unlucky," "I never get a good bounce," "I know I'm going to land in the water," "I work hard and I don't get anywhere. . . ."

These golfers are beaten before they begin. To win, first, you must want to win; second, believe you will win; and third, think only positive thoughts. We create our success or failure on the course primarily by our thoughts.

There's no doubt about it, positive thinking is a big asset to a golfer. When you find yourself in a string of bogeys, for instance, you may be tempted to say, "Well, I'll just try and par this hole." But that would be wrong. Instead, you should set your sights higher: "I'm going to birdie this hole." Then you often end up—if you don't in fact birdie—at least parring.

Another place positive thinking pays off is between nines. One reason golfers let down on the back nine is because they regard the eighteen holes as two nine-hole rounds. Maybe you find yourself shooting steady golf on the first nine, attacking all the time. But comes the second nine and you get scared and suddenly begin playing defensively, trying to hang onto your score instead of trying to turn in a better second nine.

Between nines I may say to myself, "Well, Gary, you were two under par that first side. Let's see if you can go two under this side." In other words, just continue to play a positive attacking game of golf.

The same principle applies when you have a chip shot from off the green. This is the time a lot of golfers say to themselves, "I'm going to get this chip close enough for one putt."

But that's the wrong attitude. You should say, "I'm going to try to sink it!" If you don't chip in, you'll find yourself pretty close. It's amazing how many chip shots you will sink if you convince yourself you can hole the shot.

I always like to remember what Sid Brews, another South African golfer, used to tell me. "There's only one way to play golf," Sid said. "You should try to birdie every single hole on the golf course." And Sid's right. The best way to become a really good golfer is to attack on as many holes as possible. Arnold Palmer probably exemplifiies the attacking golfer better than any player I've known. He just keeps charging, always trying to chip it in—trying for the cup.

Arnold has always played to win. He'd hit into the trees, have a bad lie, and knock it out of there with a 3-wood where others would use an iron. Things like that. This is why a lot of players said Arnold was very lucky with his fast finishes. It wasn't luck; he just

Proper thinking has played a large part in the success of the professional tournament golfers pictured here. They are, at left, Peter Thomson, the conservative Australian who has won five British Opens; Arnold Palmer, center top, legendary for his final-round charges, who I feel exemplifies the attacking type of player; Jack Nicklaus, center bottom, the best golf thinker for his age I've ever encountered. Top right, Ben Hogan, whose intense concentration allows him to eliminate from his mind all thoughts except those dealing positively with his game, and Doug Ford, bottom right, whose great positive attitude has been revealed by his ability to escape from trouble and by his consistent in-the-money record.

charged more than the rest of us did, and took more chances, thinking he could make it and actually making it because he believed in himself.

Of course, there is another side to the story. Many of the greats of golf don't continually charge or attack. But such champion golfers as Doug Ford, Peter Thomson, Ben Hogan, and especially Jack Nicklaus, are still intellectually involved in the game.

You have to think while you're playing, because thinking is concentration. Many golfers feel they shouldn't think while swinging, but I always try to think several positive thoughts simultaneously as I swing. During the backswing I'm thinking about taking the club back with both hands in "one piece." And on the downswing, I'm remembering to get that left side out of the way. But most important of all, I'm visualizing how that shot should look in flight.

But it's important not to think about future shots, except of course to consider the position you need for the shot immediately following. It's a bad mistake to be thinking about holes or specific shots beyond that, and it's easy to slip into this error. You're playing along and say to yourself, "Now I'll try and get three pars and then birdies on the sixteenth and seventeenth." Don't! It is best to play the shot and hole at hand as best you can and not even think about the others until you get to them.

It's also tough to avoid letting down mentally after you've had a good hole, especially if you have been going along with four or five pars and a couple of birdies; the tendency is to relax a little, to let up on the concentration. But you must retain your positive attitude and keep attacking even when things are going well.

You must keep your thinking positive, too, when you're up against a badly maintained course. When you face a course in bad condition the temptation is to complain. Don't! Complaining won't improve the course, and it certainly doesn't help your game. Walter Hagen had the best outlook toward this problem: he never worried or complained. He knew he had to play the course and that his competitors had to play the same course, so he went out and played it to the best of his ability. This is a philosophy I continually try to follow.

At Indianapolis one year I said, "There's no way I could win on a golf course like this! The fairway grass is too long—all I'm doing during practice is hitting 'fliers.' There's no way you can control the ball!" I made the double mistake of saying this to newspaper reporters. The next morning I read my words—and so did everyone else.

Lying in bed that night before the tournament, however, I realized I'd been doing my best all day to talk myself out of winning, so I decided to change my thinking. "I'm going to win this tournament!" I told myself. "I love to play from these kinds of lies." Thanks largely to this change in my attitude, I did win the tournament.

The player who has confidence that he has chosen the correct club for any particular shot will most likely bring it off. But to have such assurance, a golfer must know two things: how far he can hit with every club and how far he is from the target. Knowledge of the first can come only through serious practice. Make a definite point of finding out what you can do with each club, and remember it when you play.

There are two ways to ascertain how far you are

from the target. Many professional tournament golfers, including myself, "chart" a course in practice, making note of certain landmarks along the way. The weekend golfer can chart his own course easily, since he plays it regularly.

But if he's on a strange course, the player has no previous experience to guide him, and the "progression" system of distance judging can be put to use. First, pick out a tree or other landmark that is 9-iron distance down the fairway. Next, select other points in 10-yard increments, farther down the fairway, until you've reached a landmark that is even with the target. Adding one "more" club for each 10 yards, you'll know exactly what club to use for the actual shot.

Superstition can be a positive force for better golf, but you've got to be very sure you don't lose this confidence by believing your lucky charm has let you down when your game starts to go sour.

I don't wear black as a superstition; I wear it because it's my trademark. Some players wear certain colors superstitiously, and to me that's bad. A lot of people have a superstition about the number thirteen. I don't believe in that kind of nonsense. If I did, it could really upset me very much indeed.

Sometimes the people around you can bolster your confidence. Ernest Nipper, my Masters caddie at Augusta, is a good example. He played an important part in helping me win the 1961 Masters.

Whenever I arrive at Augusta, Ernest always says, "Mr. Player, we're going to win the tournament this year!" Just looking at Ernest's lovely smile makes me feel two strokes better to begin with.

In the 1962 Masters I was six behind Palmer with fifteen holes left to play. Ernest said, "You know

Caddie Ernest Nipper helped bolster my confidence during the Masters.

what? You're still going to win this thing." And I made up seven shots on Palmer in eight holes. In fact, when I stood on the twelfth tee, I was ahead. It was absolutely amazing. The confidence of my caddie gave me confidence in myself.

At the 1961 Masters, I had a putt at the 4th hole. Ernest and I were standing side by side looking at it. I thought the putt should be played to the left edge of the hole, but Ernest said, "No, Mr. Player, hit to the right edge." I hit it where he told me to and it went in. As it happened, I won the Masters by one stroke. You can't help developing confidence from a man like that.

But the people who didn't believe in me—like some people back home in South Africa, who never thought I would make it as a golfer, and said so to my face and behind my back—are probably more responsible for my success than any other factor.

By not believing in me, they all gave me the necessary determination to devote all my youthful energies to proving them wrong. They gave me the incentive I needed to concentrate almost all my early thinking and free time to perfecting my golfing technique. Instead of scuttling my confidence, those who laughed made me all the more positive I could and would one day become a champion.

As I said earlier, what we think while playing golf is probably the single most important part of any player's game.

4

BETTER GOLF THROUGH
SOUND PRACTICE

You have to work darn hard to become a "natural" golfer, but the more you practice and work, the more natural your swing will appear. Sam Snead is as natural a player as ever walked a course. But Snead, now in his fifties, still spends long hours practicing—and he always has. So there are no natural champions. Each has had to learn his trade through hours of methodical practice. Some beginning golfers do start with more natural ability than others, but never with enough to become proficient without extensive practice. The shag bag is a golfer's—especially the beginner's—best friend.

Only through practice can a golfer develop the all-important ability to repeat the same swing, shot after shot. Without a repeating swing you can't expect consistent shot results.

I remember watching Dow Finsterwald swinging

away on the practice tee just after he'd shot a sizzling 66 at Wilmington, North Carolina.

"Dow," I asked, "why in the world are you practicing now?"

"I don't want to lose it, Gary," Dow explained. "I want to keep this swing." It's something like being a businessman—he doesn't quit working just because he's had some success. A good golfer doesn't quit practicing when he's ahead.

If there is one subject in this book that I feel particularly qualified to discuss, it is practicing. During my early years in golf, I hit just about as many shots as it is possible for a human being to hit.

The first thing to stress about practice is the importance of hitting balls before you play a round. This pre-round workout is especially important for so-called weekend golfers. Remember, you can prevent a lot of pulled muscles if you warm up properly. More important, you actually improve your rhythm during a pre-round practice session. You'll be less likely to start the round with one of those bogey strings that can put you on the defensive for the rest of the day.

Naturally, you shouldn't start any practice session by hitting drives. Watch a cat slowly awaken and begin to move in the morning. He knows instinctively that stiff muscles mustn't be severely stretched.

When I was playing in the 1958 Canada Cup Matches in Japan, my tee time was about thirty minutes away and I was on the practice tee talking to some of the players. I had lost all awareness of time when suddenly they were paging me to come to the first tee. I foolishly grabbed my driver, hit three quick shots and pulled a neck muscle. It was very stupid. A boxer warms up; so does a runner or a pitcher. So should a golfer. The twisting and stretching of muscles on a full tee shot is really violent exercise.

The specific pre-round practice routine I recommend is to first head for the putting green. After you've found your swing rhythm by stroking putts, then start chipping, play a few trap shots, and finally move over to the practice tee. There, start with your short irons and work up to the woods.

Some golfers prefer to work up to their driver during pre-round practice and then try to duplicate that shot on the first tee. Others like to finish practicing by recovering their short-game touch on and around the practice putting green. You will have to determine which conclusion to your pre-round practice puts you in best shape for the first hole.

Pre-round practice, then, is vital for any golfer. So is making your practice sessions interesting. Don't allow practice to become boring. Practice won't do you much good if you're not interested in what you're doing. In fact, you'll usually be harming your game by just trying to get the session over with.

To build variety into my practice, I like to hit balls out of buried lies and from downhill and uphill slopes. I might try chip shots out of rough and hit shots over trees. Then I practice hooking or slicing around a tree, getting the particular feel of each shot as I make it (good drill for the more advanced player.) However, average golfers will find it time better spent to devote most of their practice period to mastering more basic shots. In fact, novice players should avoid practice from bad lies because they are too likely to start chopping the ball, thereby building a host of bad faults into their swings.

If you stick pretty much to cultivating a good swing

—one you can repeat each time from good lies—
you'll be better able to play from the bad ones when
you have to.

Practicing out of rough can help improve the game
of any golfer, regardless of his ability, as well as add
variety to his sessions. Practicing from the rough
teaches you how to swing "through the ball," which
you must do or you just aren't going to get much
distance. Practice in the rough not only forces you to
stay down on shots; it also strengthens your golf
muscles.

Regardless of where you happen to be practicing,
always have a target. A target sharpens your concentration, gives you a guide to judge your success or
failure, and helps spark interest. Select a tree or something else in the distance, such as a chimney, for your
target; or use your caddie if you happen to have one.

There is one story of dubious authenticity that con-
cerns Byron Nelson. It seems that Nelson, one of the
straightest shooters who ever stepped up to a tee, was
busy one day practicing his drives, using his caddie
for a target. They say one of his shots hit the caddie
—and before the lad could get up, Byron had hit him
three more times!

While failure to select a target lessens the value of
your practice, rushing shots actually hurts your game.
Too often golfers throw down a bucket of balls and
hit one shot after another with hardly a pause—or a
thought. Rushing your swing this way on the practice tee is the best way I know to destroy your rhythm
and to groove faults. If you put your shag balls behind you, you will force yourself actually to turn
around between shots—good insurance against rushing your practice.

Practice time should be put to good use, not just aimless swinging. Here I have placed a club on the ground to check my stance alignment.

To make practice sessions truly worthwhile, make certain that you're not just standing up there "perfecting your imperfections." When practicing to correct a fault, first define the problem and the correction you wish to employ.

A second person can help you overcome the basic problem that all golfers face when working on their games—the inability to see themselves swing and thus to spot faults. So often even a good player will think he's practicing a certain movement he's really not doing at all. A good observer, particularly a competent professional, can often spot a fault and prescribe a solution in minutes; he can save you hours of worthless practice. How much is an hour of your time worth? I suspect you will save money (you'll certainly save energy) by working with a pro when you have a problem.

I overcome the problem of being unable to see myself by having movies taken of my swing. Often I use a Polaroid camera while I'm practicing so I can make an immediate assessment of my faults.

Though I've been discussing practice area methods and techniques primarily, I should also point out that you can improve your skills immeasurably by practicing "on the course," or even at home.

Golfers who usually play the same course week after week may wish to try a practice technique I often use, one that helps me develop shots I normally might not encounter during the round. Say I'm playing a par-4 hole that usually requires a drive and a 7-iron. To improve my skill with other clubs, and to add variety to my round, I might tee off instead with a 2-iron and approach with a 4-iron.

Another way to improve on the course is to "play your partner's game." You select the clubs for your playing companion, tell him where to aim, how to play a putt, and so on. He does the same for you. It's fun, as well as a great way to improve your own concentration.

A big problem facing the average weekend golfer is that of preserving his swing and his touch during the week. It's here that practice at home can be extremely helpful.

I know a teaching pro in South Africa who comes home after spending most of the day on the course and practices putting on his living-room carpet. He putts to an ashtray for direction. Then, for feel, he putts to a piece of string at the far end of the carpet, trying to stop the ball at the string.

I'd strongly suggest that you too join the legion of golfers who use their putters in their living rooms.

Or, while your dinner is being prepared, take a club and swing a few times in the backyard. Even though you may not be swinging at a definite object, you should still practice swinging back slowly, then hitting "through the ball." Some golfers favor a weighted club for backyard swinging—usually a driver with a lot of lead in the head. These are readily available in most pro shops or you can do it yourself by taping lead strips on the back of one of your old woods.

This working out at home really pays off. When the weekend arrives, even though you haven't been to the course for a practice session, you will still have the feel of the club. You won't walk out on the course feeling like an arthritic gravedigger trying to swing a pickax.

It's a good idea to practice a few shots from the rough, so when you get off the fairway in actual play you'll have an idea of how to make them.

PRACTICE TIPS FROM GARY PLAYER

I. Pre-round Practice

    A. Always warm up before a game, to improve your rhythm and to prevent strained muscles.

    B. Start by putting, then chipping, before going to the practice tee.

    C. On the practice tee start with short-iron shots and work up to the woods.

II. General Practice

    A. Force yourself to pause between shots. Never rush through practice.

    B. Strive for a repeating swing.

    C. Seek professional advice, especially when correcting a fault. Don't "perfect imperfection."

    D. Always aim for a target.

    E. Spend some time during each session practicing out of rough and sand.

    F. Remember that photographs and movies will help you detect faults and correct them properly.

    G. Practice putting and club-swinging at home if you are a weekend golfer.

5

PROPER GRIP FOR CONSISTENT SHOTS

The grip is the foundation of your swing. It affects directly the position of your clubhead both throughout your swing and, more important, during impact. Without a proper grip, no golfer can expect to hit accurate shots with even a fair degree of consistency. I learned this the hard way.

When I first started golf I hooked terribly because of a bad grip—my left hand was turned so far over to the right on the club that I could see four knuckles as I looked down at it at address. My right hand was also turned to the right under the club.

In England one year I watched Dai Rees. His left hand was positioned way over to the left. That's when I decided to change my own grip. But I went to the other extreme. I exaggerated positioning my left hand to the left until I could see no knuckles at all on this hand at address.

This "weak" grip made my backswing very flat.

Although I played by gripping the club in this fashion for several years, I eventually had to change because it was such a weak position. I found that I could not reach the par-5 holes at Augusta National in two shots, and therefore left myself little chance of winning the Masters. Furthermore, this grip was putting so much pressure on my back that it hurt; since changing to my present grip I have had no more back trouble. This points up how important the grip really is.

There are several styles of gripping the club. Art Wall and Bob Rosburg, for example, use the "baseball" or "full-finger" grip. Jack Nicklaus uses the interlocking style.

Most of the pros—I'd say 99 per cent—use the Vardon overlap grip. I like the overlap grip because it's so compact. It unifies the hands in a minimum amount of space on the club, yet provides the firmness most golfers need for club control.

Use whichever grip seems most comfortable and beneficial to you. Just remember that the proper grip ties your hands closely together and keeps them working as a unit to achieve maximum power and club control.

HOW THE GRIP AFFECTS YOUR SWING

To hit accurate shots your clubface must be pointing directly at the target during impact. This is called a "square" clubface position.

To combine accuracy with maximum power, you need not only a square clubface at impact but also a similar hand alignment. The back of your left hand and palm of your right should be facing more or less toward the target. The ideal impact position is one in which the clubface looks at the target and the palms of each hand face one another in alignment with the clubface. Obviously, the best way to reach this impact position is to duplicate it at address—grip with palms facing each other and in alignment with a square clubface.

If you grip with your hands turned to the right on the shaft in what is called a "strong" grip, you cannot return to your ideal hand position at impact without turning your hands to the left during the downswing. This, of course, also turns the clubhead to the left, and the result is hooked shots.

If, at address, your hands are too far to the left in a "weak" grip, you must turn them to the right in your swing to reach an ideal impact position. This turns the clubface to the right and causes slices.

I repeat: For maximum accuracy and distance your hands at address should duplicate their ideal position at impact—palms facing each other and aligned with a square clubface.

ASSUMING THE PROPER GRIP

The first step in forming a proper grip is to rest your driver against your belt buckle and stand with your hands at your sides with palms facing inward. Next move your hands and arms forward; then place them alongside the clubshaft with the palms still facing each other.

With your hands against the club in this manner, the shaft should run diagonally across the fingers and palm of your left hand—the higher hand on the club if

proper

ADDRESS POSITIONS

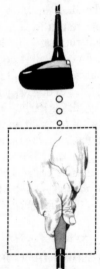

When proper grip at address returns the hands to the proper impact position, the clubface remains square to the line of flight. When strong or weak grips return hands to the proper impact position, the clubface will be turned left (closed) or right (open).

IMPACT POSITIONS

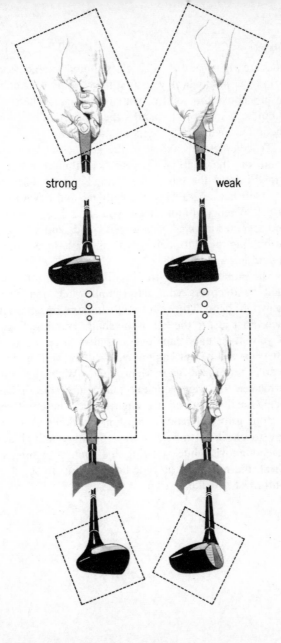

strong   weak

you are right-handed. The club should extend from below the joint where your first finger joins your palm to just above this joint of your little finger. The shaft should cross your right hand—the lower hand—across the joints where your fingers join the palm.

To complete formation of the grip, close your left hand on the shaft with your left thumb running straight down the top of the shaft. Keep the back of your left hand parallel to the clubface and toward the target. When you look down, you should see the first and second knuckles of your left hand, and you will be holding the club mainly with the last three fingers of your left hand.

The cup formed by the thumb and palm of your right hand covers your left thumb when you close your right hand. The right thumb and first finger touch each other just to the left of the shaft. The little finger of your right hand laps over the first finger of your left. You will be holding the club chiefly with the two middle fingers of your right hand. With the grip formed in this way, your two palms are more or less facing each other and are aligned with the clubface.

Your grip will require constant checking. A good way to check is to follow the gripping method described above while standing in front of a mirror. Check the reflection of your finished grip to see if it conforms to the illustrations.

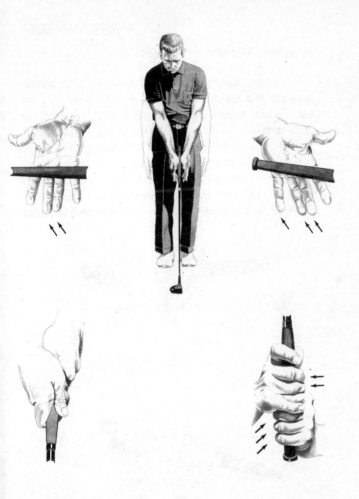

To assume proper grip, bring hands up to shaft, palms facing each other. Club lies across right hand as shown at upper left, and across left hand as shown at upper right. Complete grip is shown from front and back views at lower left and right. "Pressure fingers" are indicated by arrows.

OBTAINING PROPER GRIP PRESSURE

As I have noted, you should hold the club chiefly with the last three fingers of your left hand and the two middle fingers of your right hand. The pressure in these fingers need not be extreme, but it needs to be sufficient to hold the club firmly. Proper grip pressure is necessary for club control and a smooth swing.

A firm grasp on the shaft with your pressure fingers will keep the club from turning in your hands, especially at the top of the backswing, where club slippage

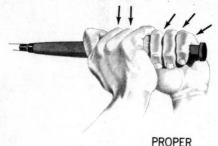

PROPER

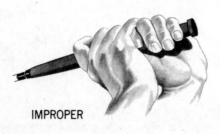

IMPROPER

Maintaining pressure in key fingers (indicated by arrows) enables you to maintain club control during backswing. Loosening of grip at top of backswing causes you to regrip; loss of control, rhythm, and timing result.

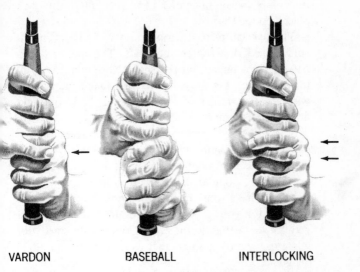

| VARDON | BASEBALL | INTERLOCKING |

Vardon overlap grip, the most common, finds seven fingers on shaft, one off. Interlocking grip has six fingers on shaft, two off. Full-finger "baseball" grip has all eight fingers on. Fingers off shaft are indicated by arrows.

most frequently occurs. If the club does slip, you must regrip during your swing. Since it is impossible to regrip in exactly the same position you originally had employed, your clubface usually becomes misaligned, your swing plane altered, and your swing rhythm destroyed.

SELECTING THE BEST GRIP FOR YOU

The essential difference among the three main styles of grips—Vardon overlap, interlock, and full-finger—is the number of fingers (excluding thumbs) placed on the shaft.

The overlap grip, described above, finds seven fingers placed directly on the shaft. The baseball grip has all eight fingers on the shaft. The interlock grip, in which the little finger of the right hand intertwines with the first finger of the left hand, finds only six fingers directly on the shaft.

The full-finger grip, with all eight fingers on the club, gives maximum club control but does not unify the hands as well as do the other grips. The full-finger grip is more popular among women and with men or boys who have weak hands. This grip is often recommended for young beginners, for it seems a natural way for them to hold the club. Golfers who start with this grip usually go to another as they begin to master the game.

The interlock grip is good for players who have small hands. An important factor in having a proper grip is to insure that the hands are closely unified. The interlocking grip effects this unification but may not give the average player sufficient club control because it places only six fingers on the shaft.

The grip you pick should depend on your individual characteristics and needs. No two golfer's hands are exactly the same size and shape, so it is impossible to recommend a specific grip for all readers. Ask a pro to suggest the best grip for you if you are a beginning player, if you think you may not be gripping the club correctly, or if you feel you are not getting optimum results from your present grip.

6

HOW TO STAND
FOR ACCURACY AND DISTANCE

If some genie were to allow me one wish that had to do with my golf game, I know what my request would be. I'd simply ask for a good swing that repeated itself every time. A consistent swing that never left its "groove" would allow me to hit shot after shot along the same flight path. A good consistent swing is the goal of every golfer.

As we have discussed, one way to achieve a high degree of consistency in your swing is through a proper grip. Another way to keep your swing in the groove, as we will see in this chapter, is through proper and consistent posture and alignment at address.

Your posture and alignment directly affect the plane of your swing and thus the path of your clubhead. If your clubhead moves along the same path each time, your shots will be consistent. However, posture and

alignment determine more than merely the plane of
your swing. They also affect your ability to turn properly, shift weight, and retain balance during your
swing. Posture and alignment therefore also affect shot
distance.

It is very easy even for accomplished golfers to be
deceived into aligning their feet and bodies improperly at address. Other professionals sometimes tell me
they are playing badly, and I ask them to hit a shot.
Often I find that they are aiming as much as 50 yards
to the right, or 20 yards to the left, of their target.

These players can't believe they are misaligned—
until I show them. It's very easy to move out of proper
alignment during the course of a season; it happens
so gradually that you may continue to feel comfortable even though you are badly misaligned.

The professionals constantly check their address
position while practicing. Jack Nicklaus and Phil
Rodgers, for example, invariably put a club across
their toes to make sure they are aligned parallel to the
target line. When I practice, I often ask one of my
friends, "Where am I aiming?"

Address position has to be checked constantly. If
the pros do this, a weekend player should too.

HOW YOUR ADDRESS POSITION AFFECTS
SHOT DIRECTION

To hit your ball to a predetermined spot, you have
to aim correctly. If the ball is to fly toward your target, your clubface must be looking at the target and
traveling along the target line during impact.

For your clubface to be looking down and moving

along the target line during impact, assume a "square" position at address. When you are square at address, lines across your toes, and through your hips and shoulders, will parallel the line from the target through the ball. This is called a square stance because you are facing at a right angle to the target line.

If your address position is square, your clubhead should move practically straight back from the ball during the start of your backswing and return similarly into the ball as it moves through the hitting area. This is obviously somewhat theoretical. If your grip is bad or if your backswing is unsound, you will not always return the clubhead squarely to the ball along the target line. However, I do feel strongly that a square address position gives most golfers their best chance of getting good shot direction.

If your address position is "closed" rather than square, the lines across your toes, hips, and shoulders point to the right of your target. From a closed address position you can hit shots either to the left or to the right. But most often a closed stance will cause your shots to go to the left—even though you are aligned (turned) to your right. Golf is a game of opposites.

A closed address position usually causes shots to go to the left for two reasons. Both causes stem from the basic fact that a golfer who is closed at address will take his club back more around his body, "inside" the target line, than is normal on his backswing. If downswing follows the same plane as backswing, the clubhead will move across the target line, away from the golfer, during impact. This imparts a counterclockwise (right-to-left) spin that causes the shot to curve left.

Some golfers take the club back on the inside and

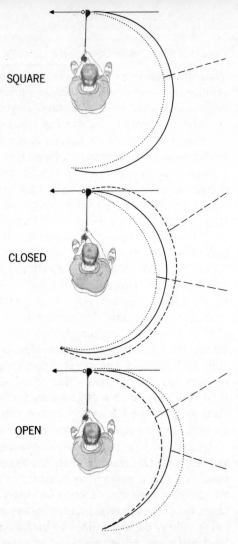

SQUARE

CLOSED

OPEN

Illustrations show how address position affects short direction. Solid lines show clubhead paths on backswings from
various positions. Other lines show most frequent downswing
paths and resulting clubhead movement in the hitting area.
Square address position finds clubhead moving along target
line in hitting area and producing straight shots. From closed

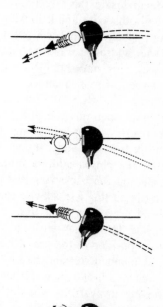

position, the clubhead will move into ball from either outside (dashed line) or extreme inside (dotted line) of target line and cause pulled or hooked shots to the left. Open address position causes clubhead to return to ball either from the extreme inside (dashed line) or outside (dotted line) of target line, so that pushed or sliced shots to the right will result. Closed position usually causes shots to fly to left of target, open position to the right.

then realize subconsciously that they are out of position to return the clubhead along the target line straight into the ball. So they throw the club to the outside on their downswing. The clubhead moves from outside to inside the target line. If the clubhead is moving in this path and is looking to the left of target during impact, the shot will pull to the left.

If your address position is "open," the lines across your toes, hips, and shoulders will point to the left of your target. An open address position usually produces shots that fly to the right of target.

From an open position, the golfer is most likely to make a very upright backswing. The club moves out and away from his body, instead of around his body as from the closed address position. With his club "outside" on the backswing, the golfer may slice the shot by imparting a clockwise spin to the ball as the clubhead moves across it from outside to inside the target line. Or he may push the shot if he realizes he is out of position at the top of his backswing. In that case, he compensates and returns the clubhead to the ball from well inside the target line. The clubhead will be moving away from him during impact and will push the shot to the right, if the clubface is looking in that direction.

Because, as we have seen, a closed address position tends to cause shots to go left and an open position flies shots to the right, slicers who aim to the left and hookers who aim to the right only aggravate their problem. A slicer who aims to the left to "play" for his slice is, in effect, opening his address position, which usually causes an even greater slice. The opposite is the case for the hooker who aims to the right.

It is much wiser to start with a square address posi-

Illustrations show proper address position. At right, I spread my feet shoulder-width apart, with pressure moving down the inside of the legs to the insteps. My right knee is slightly pre-cocked and my right elbow close to my side. At left, I bend slightly from knees and hips, as if starting to sit down on an imaginary seat stick. There is practically no bend in my back.

tion. If you hook or slice from a square position, you should look for the cause of the problem in your grip or your swing. Don't compound the error by assuming an incorrect address position.

HOW TO ASSUME SQUARE ALIGNMENT

It is a good idea to have someone else check your alignment periodically. There are also some fairly simple procedures you yourself can follow to assure you are "square" at address.

As you walk up to the ball in the fairway, draw an imaginary line from the ball to the target. Then imagine another line, at a 90-degree angle to the target line, that "extends" from the ball to an object at the right side of the fairway. When you address the ball, merely face the object at the side of the fairway and you will be square to the target line.

On the practice tee you can place a club on the ground across your toes as you address a shot. Then step back and check to see if the club lies parallel to the target line. If it does, your stance is square. On this tee it is normal to shoot from the same target on each shot. This can be a bit misleading, because in actual play your target varies each time. I suggest you also vary your target as you practice, again checking your alignment with each new target. Soon you will develop a "feel" for a square address position, regardless of the target.

HOW TO ASSUME PROPER POSTURE AT ADDRESS

The posture you assume at address is as important as your alignment. Proper posture is vital if you are to use your leg and body muscles to best advantage in a well-balanced swing movement. Golfers who do not have good posture at address waste energy that could be used to generate clubhead speed because they use so much of their effort simply keeping in balance.

The width of your stance is important. If it is too wide, it will inhibit leg action and a free hip turn. Too narrow, it will not afford the base you need to swing in balance. Ideal stance width varies with the individual. A professional will be able to tell you if yours is of proper width for your swing. Generally speaking, golfers should spread their feet—from instep to instep—about shoulder width. Weight should be distributed largely on the inside of each foot and equally between the toes and heel of each foot. Your right knee should point slightly toward the ball to "preview" its impact position.

After you have placed your feet the proper width apart and the correct distance from the ball, bend your knees slightly so that your posterior protrudes, as though you were just starting to sit down on a seat stick.

Then you should bend slightly from your waist so that you are comfortably stationed to swing at the ball. Though you bend from the waist, your spine should remain straight. Your left arm should be extended but not rigid. You should feel that your right elbow is tucked into your side—this previews the position it should be in during impact. Your over-all feeling at address should be one of "relaxed tension." You should feel firm and stable but ready to move.

WHERE TO POSITION THE BALL

Since you are striving for a consistent swing, you should position the ball in the same relative position to your feet on all *normal* shots. I generally position the ball opposite the inside of my left heel. As my stance narrows for shots with the short irons, this ball position becomes nearer stance-center—but it remains just inside my left heel.

The length and plane of your swing will vary with the length and lie of the club you're using at the time and the distance you stand from the ball. This will occur naturally, without any conscious effort on your part. To vary the ball position would require a conscious alteration in your swing, and I feel it unwise to vary the swing consciously except under abnormal conditions.

A golfer's swing plane determines how far he should stand from the ball. Tall golfers, like Al Geiberger, who tend to have very upright swings, must stand relatively close to the ball. Those with flatter swings, like mine, must stand farther from the ball.

7

HOW TO START YOUR SWING

Some months before he won the 1964 U.S. Open, Ken Venturi was playing simply awful golf—almost shamefully bad for a man of his vast talent. Ken's major fault appeared during the first few inches of his backswing, that area of the swing known as the "takeaway." He was snatching the club back so fast that it was ruining his timing; he wasn't getting a gradual buildup of potential clubhead speed that he could unleash in the hitting area.

Byron Nelson told Ken to slow down his backswing, and Ken started this slowing-down process in his takeaway. I think a slower takeaway was largely responsible for bringing Ken back onto his game.

Some golfers have been successful despite a poor takeaway. Bobby Locke violated some of the principles of the takeaway by moving his clubhead "inside" the target line very quickly. He seemed actually to brush the right side pocket of his knickers with his hands on the way back. As a result Locke, although a great player—four-time British Open champion—always had to allow for a pronounced hook. Great as Locke was, he would have been better with a good takeaway.

I find in talking with golfers of all types that while the playing professionals give considerable thought to the takeaway, the average high-handicap player seldom thinks about it. This is particularly unfortunate, because a good takeaway can do wonders for the swing of an average golfer. Players who are not particularly well coordinated have a great inclination to jerk the club back and lift it abruptly. As soon as I tell them to take the club back slowly and smoothly, they automatically improve their swings.

A lesson on the takeaway, besides being valuable in itself, has the further virtue of being simple to put across and easy to understand. The player can see and quickly grasp what he is doing on his takeaway. This is not always the case on other phases of the swing— on the latter stages of the backswing, for instance, when the clubhead is out of the player's field of vision.

Mastering the takeaway helps golfers grasp the concept of producing maximum clubhead speed at impact—the idea of gradual acceleration into the hitting area. In learning a proper takeaway the golfer begins to realize that there is no need for high-speed action in the pre-hitting stages of the swing and that, in fact, such action is highly detrimental.

What you have to do is try to think the swing through, with the takeaway as the starting point. As you address the ball for a shot, have a clear mental picture of a fluid, smooth, unhurried, rhythmical take-

Proper takeaway of clubhead from the ball puts hands in good position at top of backswing (center dashed line). Improper takeaway movements (left and right dashed lines) force hands to move out of their backswing path at top of swing in order to arrive at correct position to start downswing.

away of the clubhead from the ball. Then convert the mental picture into actuality.

In subsequent chapters we will discuss the backswing turn, the position at the top of the backswing, and so on through to the finish of the swing. Meanwhile, I hope you will have mastered the basics of the takeaway—the first 12 inches or so of clubhead movement from the ball. Then you can integrate it into the swing pattern as a whole. You will see how a correct takeaway leads to a better understanding and mastery of the other phases of the swing—just as a correct grip and stance, as we have seen, make it easier to produce a proper takeaway.

The idea in developing a golf swing is to do as many things correctly as you can, progressively. One good move leads to the next. And one bad move can ruin the whole thing.

As an example of how one good thing in a golf swing leads to another, note that when you make a correct takeaway you naturally keep your left arm straight and fully extended—it happens automatically. And the fully extended left arm is the basis of a wide, full swing arc.

As Ben Hogan once said, the golf swing is sort of like making a Western movie. If you set it up so the good guys can take over, the bad ones can't.

PROPER TAKEAWAY PATH

The backswing as a whole finds the clubhead not only raising as the shoulders tilt, but also moving around "inside" the target line as the shoulders turn.

However, the movement of the clubhead to the inside should be hardly perceptible during the takeaway. In a proper takeaway the clubhead should *appear* to be moving straight back from the ball, along the target line. Taking the clubhead straight back for about 12 inches sets your swing for a long clubhead arc. It gives your backswing good "width," because such a takeaway cannot be achieved without an extended left arm. The long clubhead arc that begins with a "straight" takeaway is a prime source of power.

If you wanted to throw a ball softly, a short arc would suffice. Or think of clapping your hands. Bring the hands only 2 inches apart and you are capable of generating little "clap." Widen the space to 6 inches and you can triple your power (hand speed). So it is in golf. The more you increase the distance the clubhead travels, the more it can accelerate. When you see a little man who hits the ball a long way—Norman von Nida of Australia is an excellent example—you can know that he manages a wide arc despite his size. A very big man like George Bayer naturally has a big swing arc.

Starting the clubhead back straight from the ball not only sets up a nice wide backswing, it also puts the clubhead on a proper path. The golfer need not loop the club at the top of his swing to bring it into the proper position to start the downswing. With a proper takeaway you won't have to adjust for error before starting down. You can keep your swing a simple, "one-piece" affair.

PROPER TAKEAWAY TEMPO

Takeaway tempo is as important as takeaway path. The takeaway should be smooth, unhurried, fluid, rhythmic—the qualities you want in the over-all swing. And the takeaway is the place to set the tempo. It is possible for a swing that started smoothly to degenerate into something frantic and jerky before its completion. But you have no chance at all to achieve over-all smoothness if you snatch the club back abruptly at the start.

A smooth takeaway tempo is additionally important because you want to conserve your strength and energy on the backswing. The place to expand your strength and energy is on your downswing, particularly during impact. (Talking about the need for a nice smooth, unhurried takeaway makes the truth and logic of it come to me with great clarity. How I wish I could always remember this principle on the golf course!)

HOW TO EXECUTE THE TAKEAWAY

Although the takeaway may appear to be strictly a hand-arm movement, it isn't. Actually, the takeaway —like the backswing as a whole—is a "one-piece" movement in which the golfer's entire body, including his hands and arms, move as a unit. Everything goes at once—you can think of this backswing movement as a real "package" deal.

The "one-piece" unified takeaway coordinates the various parts of the human body so that everything works together in a common purpose, and at the same

Large drawing shows proper takeaway flow. Note how everything moves together as a unit. If takeaway is made as a one-piece movement, golfer fully coils on the backswing as in the small illustration at right. If takeaway is made solely with hands and arms, body fails to coil as in small illustration, left.

time. The big muscles of the legs, back, and shoulders begin to stretch and coil and thus build up potential power that will later be transmitted to the clubhead. The golfer who relies solely on his hands and arms to start his backswing wastes a great portion of his potential power. He does not fully stretch those big muscles to the point that they can uncoil in a great surge of power on the downswing.

I don't think that the average golfer need consciously concern himself with the lower portion of his body when making his takeaway. If your hands and arms move back in conjunction with a turning-under of your left shoulder, your legs and hips will automatically work together correctly as a unit at the same time. You will be well on your way to a smooth one-piece swing if your clubhead moves unhurriedly straight back from the ball as a result of your left shoulder's beginning to lower under your chin. Everything will move as a unit if your left shoulder lowers properly.

HOW TO AVOID LATERAL MOVEMENT

We have seen that the clubhead should move straight back and low to the ground during the first 12 inches of the backswing. This helps provide a long clubhead arc and a full stretching of the golfer's muscles. Unfortunately, many golfers carry the low, straight takeaway to an extreme.

The 12-inch figure is arbitrary. The club should never move straight back so far that it causes the

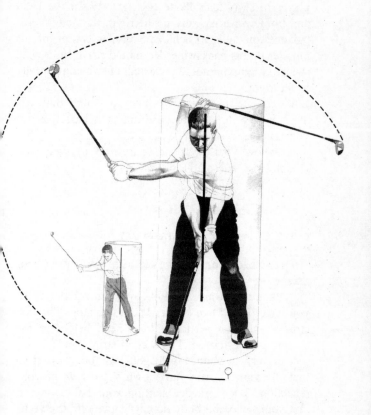

Moving clubhead straight back from ball helps provide a wide swing arc. Care must be taken so that you don't sway laterally to the right as a result. Imagine that you are swinging inside a metal drum (large drawing) and avoid touching its "inside" (smaller drawing).

player to sway laterally to his right. When the head and body move laterally to the right, the golfer loses balance and fails to achieve a proper coiling of his muscles on his backswing. He should strive for a wide swing pattern, but not to the extent of swaying laterally to the right.

Practice your takeaway while imagining that you are standing inside a metal drum or a barrel. Move your clubhead straight back, low to the ground, but don't allow your body or your head to sway and "touch" the side of the drum.

DRILLS TO IMPROVE YOUR TAKEAWAY

Here are two practice tips to help you perfect your takeaway:

1. Stand in front of a full-length mirror on which you have placed two strips of adhesive tape. The first strip should run vertically from head height to the bottom of the mirror. The second strip should intersect the first at about hip height. Position yourself so that the vertical strip runs down the center of your reflection. Then practice starting your backswing so that your head and body do not "move off" the vertical tape. Also, take the club back so that you see no "hinging" of your wrists until they have raised above the horizontal tape.

2. Place one golf ball about 12 inches directly behind another. Address the front ball, and practice making the takeaway so that your clubhead grazes the rear ball. If you sway to the right, slightly reduce the distance between the two balls.

8

HOW TO MAKE
A PROPER BACKSWING TURN

THE TURN

Now we come to the phase of the backswing called the "turn." By now you should have mastered the takeaway—the smooth, unhurried initial movement of the backswing in which you take the clubhead back from the ball in a straight line and low to the ground —and are ready to give thought to the next step.

The turn, particularly of the shoulders, actually begins with the takeaway; both are integral parts of the backswing. We deal with the takeaway and the turn separately only to give you a close look at each phase, as in a blueprint. Ultimately we shall fit all the phases together and arrive at a harmonious one-piece golf swing.

We might as accurately have called this chapter "The Windup." The turn produces the windup; it winds the body up so that at the proper stage of the swing (the start of the downswing), the body will naturally unwind, much as a coiled spring does when the pressure on it is released.

The best examples of what the turn should be include players with whose swings the golfing public is quite familiar—Sam Snead, Ben Hogan, Arnold Palmer, Bobby Locke, Byron Nelson. It is no coincidence that our examples have at one time or other been at the top of the golfing world, because a correct turn and a great golf swing are inseparable. You can't have the great swing without the correct turn.

Take Sam Snead. Now in his fifties, Snead still plays astoundingly good golf. He can do it because he has a great windup—one of the greatest I've ever seen. His rhythm is fantastic.

Approximately the same age, Ben Hogan remains one of the finest strikers of the ball anywhere; he could still be a tournament winner had he not lost his putting touch. He has a great windup, and stresses it in his own instructional writing.

Arnold Palmer, who needs no buildup from me, makes the error of having his clubface shut at the top of his backswing, but he more than gets away with it because he has a truly great shoulder turn—and because he is so very strong.

If you were fortunate enough to have seen Byron Nelson in his prime, you will recognize that he too had a full, rhythmic turn that was beautiful to watch.

Bobby Locke, not a particularly strong man physically, owed much of his success to a fine, full shoulder turn.

We can also add Jack Nicklaus. It goes without saying that he has a great shoulder turn. The golf ball

Proper shoulder turn on backswing fully coils the back muscles as if they were a spring. Golfer's back will be facing the target at the top of his backswing. Uncoiling on downswing produces proper clubhead speed.

just can't be hit as far as Jack hits it with any sort of a restricted turn.

One good thing in the golf swing leads naturally to another. In this case, the correct turn leads to a correct and power-loaded position at the top of the backswing. A good backswing turn makes it natural for you to start the downswing as you should—smoothly, with the hands trailing so as to release their power at the right time, which is just as the clubhead is coming into the ball. By the same token, the correct turn inhibits the swing-wrecking error of starting the downswing with the hands dominating the action—hitting from the top, casting, or whatever you choose to call it.

TURN SHOULDERS TO THE MAXIMUM

Let's look first at what a correct turn accomplishes.

A correct turn brings the shoulders around to the maximum—without undue strain, of course. Ideally, the left shoulder will move under the chin, and the back will be facing the target at the completion of the turn. The shoulder and back muscles, and the muscles controlling the movement of the hips, will be stretched taut—not strained, just stretched and ready to react in the opposite direction to produce a powerfu! downswing.

You want this full shoulder turn not only because it gives you a complete backswing, but also because it gives you a repeating backswing. With a full shoulder turn you can reach the same top-of-the-backswing position each time. If your shoulder turn varies, your backswing will be inconsistent. You will be starting

I follow the modern trend in backswing turns, with my shoulders winding up to a much greater degree than my hips. The difference in degree of turn produces additional coiling of the back muscles.

your downswing from varying positions—and you can't play good consistent golf that way.

TURN SHOULDERS MORE THAN HIPS

You will notice that I emphasize the shoulder turn to the near-exclusion of the hip turn. If the shoulder turn is made correctly, the hip turn will take care of itself.

It is an inescapable physical fact that in a proper backswing the shoulders must turn farther around than the hips—about twice as far, at least. It is the relative degree of shoulder and hip turn that produces the muscle stretching for a maximum buildup of potential force.

There are those who advocate consciously retarding the hip turn, the better to stretch the muscles, but my view is that giving the shoulders a full turn makes it unnecessary to give thought to the hip turn. This goes back to the stance. If the stance is right, the hips will turn in the amount they should, provided only that you take a full turn with the shoulders. It will be automatic.

AVOID LATERAL MOVEMENT

To realize what the correct turn is, we have to know what it is *not*. There must be no lateral movement (sway) involved. On the backswing the body *turns,* and *only* turns, on a tilted plane as the left shoulder moves under the chin.

If .you sway laterally, the head moves. Thus the

hub of the swing changes position, throwing your club out of a proper path; you will not achieve the coiling of muscles you desire. It is senseless to try to get your left shoulder to move under your chin, as it should, when your head is moving all over the place. You will know well and quickly when you sway. The swing will feel sloppy, instead of giving you the nice firm feeling that accompanies a swing in which the head is kept steady.

One golfer who does some swaying is Chi Chi Rodriguez. On his good swings, which are in the great majority, he makes a good turn and his head is quite steady. But on his occasional bad swings, he sways. The contrast in his shot results clearly defines the need for turning and not swaying. Rodriguez is a tremendously talented player for his slight build, but he doesn't play consistently enough yet because of this sway. If I were Chi Chi, I would concentrate on hitting the ball straighter more consistently, and when I really needed the length, I'd let it out. But Chi Chi is inclined to let it out on every single drive.

BRUSH CHIN WITH LEFT SHOULDER

For most golfers there is a simple guide to knowing when they have accomplished a full shoulder turn. The top of their left shoulder will brush the tip of their chin at the top of their backswing. If the golfer is extraordinarily supple, as in the unusual case of Sam Snead, the left shoulder may move past and well under the tip of the chin. Such a golfer's back may be facing to the right of the target, instead of directly toward it, at the top of his backswing. But the bigger

The shoulders must turn on a tilted plane in the golf swing because you are striking a ball that is at ground level. Avoid a level-shoulder turn that would be more suitable for a baseball player swinging at a chest-high pitch.

To increase your backswing shoulder turn, I suggest this exercise: Start with a 10-pound dumbbell, place it behind your neck, and hold the ends of the weight with your hands. Now, simulate a backswing turn. This will strengthen your shoulder muscles and make them supple, and soon you can swing back with a good shoulder turn.

turn is fine; you can't overdo the shoulder turn so long as you stay in balance and retain a firm grip on the club.

Some golfers are not supple enough to turn their shoulders enough to make shoulder contact with the tip of the chin. These golfers must go altogether on feel. But there is a definite feeling when the shoulders are turned to the maximum, short of straining, and this is the feeling to develop and look for.

The point is that you want to make as full a shoulder turn as possible. A big shoulder turn is desirable, but a lesser turn will suffice so long as your muscles stretch fully.

The fact that the top of the left shoulder should touch (or nearly touch) the underside of the chin points out that the rotation of the shoulders is on an inclined plane. In a flat, baseball-type swing, of course, the shoulders would turn on a horizontal plane. The plane on which the shoulders should turn in the golf swing is more nearly vertical because the object to be struck is at ground level. The exact plane of the shoulder turn is determined largely by the distance you stand from the ball.

DRILLS TO INCREASE YOUR SHOULDER TURN

There are two exercises that will help increase your shoulder turn, that will add suppleness as well as strength.

The first one I use and recommend is done with weights. I take a 30-pound dumbbell and put it behind my neck. I make my shoulder turn as I hold on to the ends of the weight with my hands. This makes me very supple and stretches my muscles, and helps me strengthen my shoulders. In years to come, I think, all top golfers will be doing weight training. The other drill is to place a golf club behind the neck, with the arms dangling loosely over it.

This is a good exercise. But it is also the exercise that just about everybody else does. And if you want to excel in golf you've got to do something special. I would suggest, therefore, that you get yourself some weights. Start with, say, a 10-pound weight, and work up. Don't try it with the 30-pound weight I use—at least not until you have strengthened yourself with the lighter weights.

9

PROPER POSITION AT THE
TOP OF THE SWING

POSITION AT THE TOP OF THE BACKSWING

The golfer's position at the top of the backswing reflects everything that has gone before—grip, stance, takeaway, turn: the whole thing. This logical and perhaps obvious statement is made as a reminder, and as a prelude to reviewing briefly what has been set out in earlier chapters.

My own experience offers an excellent illustration of the importance of the correct grip. When I was quite a young golfer I had a very, very flat swing, and hence a poor position at the top of my backswing. The trouble, I soon discovered, was in my grip. I had my left thumb far to the left-hand side of the shaft, and my right hand was also well to the left side. The inevitable result was that when I reached the top of the backswing the palm of my right hand, instead of

my left thumb, was supporting my club. I was advised
to try to swing more upright—the poorest possible
advice. All I needed was a correct grip, with my left
thumb straight down the top of the shaft. Such a grip
eventually did eliminate that very flat swing and set
me on the road to vast improvement.

As we have seen, a correct stance largely determines proper turning of the shoulders and hips. This
helps produce a top-of-the-backswing position in
which the shoulders are fully turned and the hips are
turned just enough to set up a proper muscle tension
to be released during the downswing.

A good takeaway—straight back from the ball and
low to the ground—sets the club on the path it
should take to reach the right position at the top. If
the takeaway is smooth and unhurried, you can more
easily retain balance—and thus make a correct turn
that will bring you to the top with your shoulders and
hips properly positioned.

Being in the proper position at the top of the swing
makes it so much easier to start the downswing as you
should, with the club moving along a proper path and
in a proper plane. Once the downswing is started, the
die is cast. If you have started it from an improper
position, it is very difficult to achieve consistently
accurate shots.

This is not to say that you can't play good golf
without being in the ideal position at the top. In this
connection I think immediately of Chick Harbert,
who in my opinion never took the club back correctly, but who, as the record shows, played some
great golf. Chick moved the club around quite freely
at the top of his swing, to reach a correct position for
starting the downswing—making adjustments, cor-

recting errors. Being very strong and talented, he could correct and adjust and still play well, but the average golfer could not make the compensations.

I don't think that Jack Nicklaus' position at the top is 100 per cent perfect, either. His right elbow points out, away from his body, more than it should, and he has to reposition this elbow before starting his downswing. Jack is nothing but great, of course, as his record and bulging bank account so clearly prove; it's just that I think he could be even better if he removed this flaw from his swing.

The man with the best top-of-the-backswing position I've ever seen is Ben Hogan. He is right where he should be. He has no need whatsoever to correct or adjust. He simply flows into his downswing and hits the ball solid and straight. This is why in just about every tournament he plays in, he putts for more birdies than any other man in the competition. (His problem is that he also misses a lot more birdie putts than the rest do.)

Just a couple of years ago at the Masters, Ben came into the locker room and Jack Burke asked him what he had shot.

"Seventy-three," said Ben.

"That's pretty good for a man who has to lay up on those six-footers," Jack noted.

Subsequent discussion revealed that Hogan had used thirty-six strokes to reach the greens and had taken thirty-seven putts.

Before going on to some specific tips, let me make it clear that the position at the top of the backswing is not a static thing—not something to be thought of separately and apart from the swing as a whole. The backswing should blend in smoothly with the downswing. Cary Middlecoff, when he was playing his best, stopped the club at the top for a time that seemed interminable. There can be little doubt that this delay put a big strain on his timing. He might perhaps still be consistently a winner had he developed a swing in which the transition from backswing to downswing was smoother.

LEFT THUMB SUPPORTS CLUBSHAFT

As already noted, one feature of a correct top-of-the-swing position is that the left thumb is directly under the shaft, supporting the weight of the club. This thumb position is largely taken care of in the grip. If you have a good grip, with your left thumb on top of the shaft, this thumb should be under the shaft at the top of your swing—if you have made a properly coordinated backswing.

To get the idea of this correct left-thumb position, take your normal address position and grip the club with your left thumb down the top of the shaft. Then, without straightening your body up, lift your hands until they are in front of your face. The club should be pointing straight up and the nail side of your left thumb facing you. Finally, merely turn your shoulders to the right until your club is in its top-of-the-swing position.

Your club should now be supported by your left thumb. The back of your left hand should form a continuous line with your left arm; there should be no break at the back of your left wrist. This is the proper top-of-the-swing position, from which you can move readily and smoothly into your downswing.

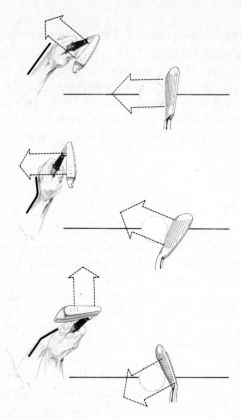

Drawings illustrate various positions at top of backswing (left) along with impact positions that would normally result (right). Top drawing shows the proper top-of-backswing position. Note that left thumb supports club, and back of wrist is straight. Such positioning gives square clubface at impact. Middle drawing shows "open" clubface position in which the left palm supports club; and wrist bows inward. This is likely to produce an open face at impact. Lower drawing shows clubface closed at top of backswing. Club is supported by golfer's right palm, and left wrist bows outward. Clubface looks skyward at top of backswing; to left, in closed position, at impact. Hooked shots to the left are likely to occur.

Your clubface will be properly aligned to return squarely to the ball.

If you find that your club is inclined to be supported by your right palm, chances are that your clubface is looking skyward. This is a "closed" clubface position and usually produces hooked shots. If your left palm seems to be slightly under the clubshaft, your clubface position is probably "open" and sliced shots will probably result.

CLUBSHAFT PARALLELS TARGET LINE

Another highly important feature point about position at the top is that the clubshaft should parallel the target line. The club's position largely tells you whether or not you have made a good backswing. If the club points to the right of the target line, you have taken the club back too much "inside" around your body; unless you make some sort of an adjustment in your downswing, you will probably hook the shot. You will either be a deliberate and consistent hooker, like Bobby Locke, or you will be fighting a hook, like Chick Harbert. It follows, of course, that the golfer whose club at the top points to the left of the target probably will be fighting a slice.

In between these extremes you have Hogan, whose club parallels the target line, and who has only to fight his putter.

The direction your club points at the top of your swing is determined largely by your takeaway. If you take the clubhead straight back for about 12 inches, the clubshaft should parallel the target at the top. If you start the club back outside the target line you can

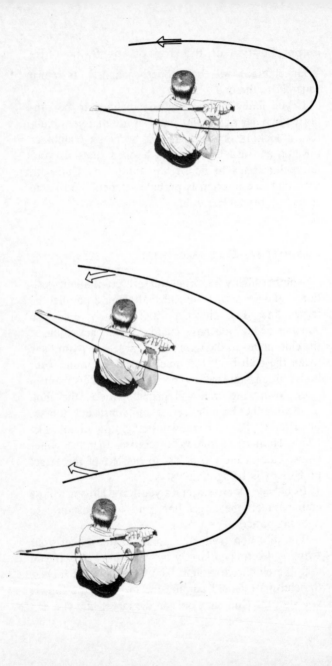

figure on reaching the top of your backswing with the club pointing to the left of your target. Start it back inside the target line and you wind up with your club pointing to the right of your target.

These latter two faults do add up to one virtue. If you need a deliberate slice, take the club back outside the line. Reverse the process if your situation calls for a deliberate hook.

PRACTICE SWINGING HEAVY CLUB

Here is one drill by which you can both check and improve your backswing, and thus arrive at a proper position at the top.

Take a very heavy golf club, not an ordinary club such as would be used in actual play, but a specially leaded one. You can buy such clubs, or merely apply lead tape to the back of an old driver. Practice swinging this club to the top of your backswing and then stopping. This will not only strengthen your fingers and wrists but will also help you check to see that you are in correct position. If you have a weakness in your grip, for instance, this drill will show it up.

These drawings illustrate how the path of your backswing will affect your shots. Ideally, the clubhead should be taken more or less straight away from the ball (top). When this happens, clubshaft parallels intended shot line and a straight shot (arrow) results. When clubhead is swung inside (center), clubshaft points to right of target at top of backswing, and a hooked shot to the left may result. When clubhead is taken back outside the intended line (bottom), clubshaft points to the left of target and a sliced shot to the right may result.

This drill is also especially good for a golfer who is inclined to have a snappy, hurried backswing. You can't snatch back a club of such a heavy weight and swing too fast.

NEVER TOO LATE TO IMPROVE

Before leaving this subject, something probably should be included for those veteran golfers who may say, "Well, I've been playing golf for more than fifteen years now and really have a bad position at the top of my backswing, but it's too late to change."

I would suggest that such golfers make every feasible effort to improve on their top-of-the-backswing position, even if they can't logically hope to achieve Hoganlike perfection. Every little bit helps.

Secondly, golfers who move into a bad position on the backswing should realize that if they are to play well they must make an extra effort on the downswing. They must compensate for backswing shortcomings by working harder to perfect downswing moves that would occur naturally if they had good position at the top.

Keep working on reaching a good (or at least a better) position at the top. It might be simpler to do than you think. Often when you can improve one phase of your swing, other areas automatically improve as a result.

10

PUTTING YOUR FEET TO WORK

FOOTWORK

Good footwork is a basic to a good golf swing, a point that can easily be proved by example. Simply list the truly great players in the history of the game—Ben Hogan, Sam Snead, Byron Nelson, Arnold Palmer, and Jack Nicklaus, to name just five outstanding ones. The swing of each is characterized by excellent foot and leg action.

Two other golfers who come to mind in this connection are Chi Chi Rodriguez and Bob Toski. Both are very small in stature, weighing scarcely more than 120 pounds, yet they hit the golf ball with exceptional power, frequently outdriving much larger men. Much of their distance originates in good footwork. Both Rodriguez and Toski are exceptionally fast on their feet, generating tremendous leg and body drive, which transmits into clubhead speed.

The point can also be proved by logic. You have to stay in balance while shifting your weight to your right side on your backswing and then quickly back to your left side at the start of your downswing. You can't shift weight quickly and still retain balance without moving your feet and legs correctly.

I was a negative example of this point during one phase of my career. I kept falling back on my right foot, failing to maintain proper balance during my downswing and follow-through. The problem and the answer, of course, was footwork. Not until I improved my footwork did I begin to play well again.

PROPER STANCE WIDTH BREEDS GOOD FOOTWORK

Good footwork begins with a good stance. The feet must be properly placed, just as the wheels of a car or a locomotive must be in the right place and correctly aligned. The stance should be wide enough to provide balance, but not so wide as to restrict freedom of movement.

As I have noted before, I feel that, for a full drive, the insteps of the feet should be as far apart as the width of the shoulders. This places the feet directly under the shoulders, the logical place for them to be to provide balanced support during the swing.

(At this point, a lot of people are going to ask about Doug Sanders. Doug indeed plays wonderfully well with a stance that is considerably wider than I advocate, but I am firmly of the opinion that he succeeds in spite of this wide stance rather than because of it. Further, he is more of a hand player than most of the other golfers on the tour.)

With right foot square to intended line of flight at address (illustration at left), a full coiling of the upper body on the backswing is encouraged, while the hip turn is somewhat restricted (large hand). With left foot turned left slightly (illustration at right), the hip turn to the left on the down-swing is free and fast (large hand "pulling" hips around).

The stance narrows as you progress to the shorter irons. Since these shots call for a shorter backswing, a slightly narrower stance will give you the balance you need, at the same time allowing the quick transition of the weight from the right side to the left side to start the downswing.

POINT TOES IN PROPER DIRECTION

Proper stance width is vital to good footwork, but so is proper foot alignment. I feel that most golfers should point the right foot directly forward, at a right angle to the target—"square," so to speak. The left foot should be turned to the left about an inch and a half, leaving the left toe pointing a bit more toward the target than the right. (The reasoning here is that on the backswing you want to achieve a full coiling of your upper body with the shoulders turning fully and the hip turn being somewhat restricted. The squared right foot will keep your hips from turning too far around. On the downswing you want the hips to move freely and fast to the left. Pointing the left toe slightly outward increases your ability to move your left hip out of the way of your arms and hands coming through.)

FIRM LEFT HEEL IMPROVES BACKSWING

If you are supple enough to keep your left heel on the ground throughout your backswing, you will derive at least three benefits:

First, you eliminate the risk of not replacing it exactly where it was at the start of the swing. Such

If you are supple enough, as I am, you should keep your left heel almost on the ground throughout the swing to help groove the swing, to create a full coil of the muscles on the backswing, and to fight a lateral sway. Those less supple can roll the left foot to the right on the backswing (center circle) and achieve good results, but never should the heel be lifted extremely high off the ground (lower circle).

misplacement can throw your whole swing pattern out of kilter because your position changes with reference to the ball.

Second, keeping the left heel on the ground helps you coil fully on your backswing, thus creating muscular tension to be released as downswing force.

Third, keeping your left heel on the ground lessens the chance that you will sway laterally to your right on your backswing. All golfers should keep the left heel planted on short iron shots. If you must raise it on longer shots, merely roll onto your instep; don't lift the entire heel and go up on your toes.

SHIFT WEIGHT TO RIGHT INSTEP

Another key to good footwork is having the bulk of your weight on the inside of your right foot at the top of your backswing. Then you can push off with the right foot to start the downswing. This gets the hips moving fast to the left as they must to generate power.

Hogan says he starts his downswing simply by turning his left hip back around to the left—but you can be sure that Hogan has the bulk of his weight on the inside of his right foot at the top of the backswing. *And* that his hip turn to the left is accompanied by a pushing-off with his right instep.

DRILLS TO IMPROVE FOOTWORK

To achieve good footwork, you've got to be light and fast on your feet. They must be active during the swing to keep the legs working as they should.

When a golfer's feet are working properly during his swing, his weight moves to the instep of the right foot during the backswing (left). By pushing off from his right foot at the start of the downswing (right), the golfer helps achieve a proper shifting of his weight to the left.

There are a number of exercises that will help you improve your footwork. One is skipping rope—the exercise boxers use so much. By skipping you develop the habit of moving your legs very quickly, and with good rhythm.

I also think knee-bends help your footwork. But be careful not to overdo this exercise—a lot of deep squats may damage the cartilage in your knees.

Running is also good, because you need stamina for those finishing holes. If you lack stamina, one of the first places you begin to tire is in the feet and lower legs. Running is good for your over-all health as well as for your golf. I strongly advise it.

Finally, I offer you a training suggestion I have used to advantage. I have a pair of weights I got in the States. They are padded and they've got a little buckshot in them. I clip these weights around my legs, then practice my swing. They're not very heavy. But I find that after I swing with these weights on my legs, then take them off, I feel that I can swing with twice the speed. It is like a broad-jumper or a high-jumper who uses weighted shoes in practice. After he changes to his regular jumping shoes, he feels he has far greater spring in his legs.

11

HOW TIMING AND RHYTHM
AFFECT YOUR SHOTS

TIMING AND RHYTHM

The essence of timing in golf is that the swing should
be arranged (timed) so that the clubhead is accelerating throughout the length of the downswing and
reaches the ball at maximum speed. On the backswing, timing implies the faculty of being able to
sense the position and speed of the clubhead when it
is out of your field of vision. Timing comes with
practice, provided you are applying the correct fundamentals of grip, stance, and the like.

Rhythm as applied to golf is perhaps best defined
as measured motion. You want your golf swing to be
smooth, sustained, flowing. You want to avoid making
it jerky, hasty, frantic. Sam Snead's swing is the
epitome of rhythm. If you have seen Snead play golf
and can picture his swing in your mind, you know

what I mean by rhythm. His rhythm is so great that it communicates itself to the people he is playing with. I love to play with Sam because I unconsciously absorb his fine rhythm into my own swing.

Whenever you see a player hit a golf ball long and straight, you are watching the results of a well-timed golf swing. This is true even though the player can hit only one or two such shots a round. The great players are the ones who can time nearly every swing perfectly; whose timing, when it is off at all, is only slightly off. On this basis, you probably would have to say that the golfer with the best timing is Ben Hogan—or, in a slightly earlier period, Byron Nelson.

Plagued as he was by recurring physical ailments and by worries stemming from them, Ken Venturi has in recent years offered a graphic illustration of the difference between having and not having rhythm and timing. During the all-too-infrequent periods when he was feeling fit and could center his mind on golf, Ken had wonderful rhythm and timing; he hit the ball as solid and straight as any man could. When he was hurting, and worrying as a consequence, his rhythm and timing left him almost completely.

PACE YOURSELF TO IMPROVE RHYTHM AND TIMING

To achieve good timing and rhythm (they are inseparable, and it doesn't matter which you mention first) and to maintain it day after day, the golfer must have another quality, which I will call "pace." Pace, as I apply it here, refers not to the actual swing but to the golfer's actions and frame of mind prior to teeing off and between shots.

My example here is Julius Boros. He is always calm, never flustered. Before the day's play begins, whether it is the last round of the U.S. Open or a routine practice round, Boros takes it easy. He dresses leisurely, strolls leisurely to the practice tee, warms up leisurely, and leisurely moves on to the first tee. Between shots he gives the appearance of being out for a pleasant walk. If he has to wait for the group ahead to clear the green, he shows not the least sign of impatience. If he hits a shot that doesn't satisfy him, he seems to shut it out of his mind completely and immediately.

Thus he is able to maintain fantastic rhythm and timing. With Boros, I think, this is all perfectly natural—part and parcel of his personality. But some of us, notably Arnold Palmer and myself, must work at achieving pace. Let me use myself as an example.

Before the 1965 U.S. Open at St. Louis, I practiced pace. For a whole week before the opening round on Thursday, and between rounds, I deliberately did things more slowly than my nature normally dictates. When I spoke to people, I spoke slowly. I didn't rush to the practice tee. I set a calm, slow pace for myself in all things—eating, dressing, going to and from the course. While there were a number of things that went into my being able to win this tournament, I think that maintaining good pace—and the good swing rhythm and timing that resulted—was one of the more important reasons.

I am aware that the average golfer can scarcely afford to spend a week in mental preparation for a golf game. But neither does he have to rush to the golf course, dash to the practice tee, and hit as many warm-up shots as he can squeeze in, fidget and fuss while waiting for the players ahead to move out of his way, and do all the other such things calculated to wreck his timing and rhythm.

A spot familiar to literally millions of golfers, either through television or from having been there personally, is an area on the 15th hole at the Augusta National Course some 260 to 280 yards out from the tee and perhaps 220 yards from the front fringe of the green. Here many players in the Masters have to make a decision whether to try to fly the ball over the pond fronting the green and set up a relatively easy birdie-4 or lag short and pretty well clinch a par-5.

There is almost always a rather long wait here for the players ahead to clear the green. Some players use this time to fidget and to wonder about trying to carry the pond. Then, when the time comes, if they have elected to try to carry the water, they snatch the club back fast and try to put something extra behind the shot. They are generally the ones who hit the water and wind up with a bogey-6, or worse. They let anxiety and lack of confidence destroy their rhythm and timing.

Other players, knowing they will have to wait to hit their second shots, deliberately slow their walking pace to reach their drives just shortly before time for their second shots. They then make a prompt and firm decision, and if that decision is to fly the pond, they swing as if there were no water hazard there—knowing that a shot hit with good timing and rhythm will give them a maximum of both distance and accuracy.

Also in connection with pace, I should mention Jack Nicklaus and my fellow countryman Bobby Locke. Nicklaus paces himself well. Locke was bothered neither by being delayed himself nor by delaying the group behind. He played at his own pace.

If you are the type of golfer who has to play four or five holes before you "settle down," think about pace.

START YOUR SWING RHYTHMICALLY

Good rhythm and timing begin as you step up to the shot. Approach the ball in a leisurely manner. Waggle the club rhythmically. Attune your body to the rhythm you want in your swing.

In the swing proper, good timing and rhythm begin with the takeaway. Start the club back slowly and smoothly. Don't snatch it away from the ball. A smooth takeaway will help you accomplish a smooth backswing. Because you must complete your backswing before you can start your downswing, there is no hurry about the backswing—still you don't want a really slow backswing. If you swing back too slowly you destroy the needed tempo and make it hard for yourself to stay in balance.

If your backswing is rhythmic, you will find it easy to stay in balance through the crucial period of transition from backswing to downswing. But if you snatch the club back fast, you naturally generate a force that tends to pull you off balance and make you sway off the ball in the direction opposite your target. It then becomes all but impossible to shift your weight to your left at the start of your downswing.

There is a good tip contained in a story told me recently by Bob Toski. He was giving a lesson to a fellow who persisted in starting his backswing with muscles all tensed and bunched, giving himself no chance for rhythm and timing.

"You look like a butcher," Bob told him. "Try to look like a surgeon."

"Would you believe it? I am a surgeon!" the fellow said.

"Well," said Bob, "would you try to operate when you were all tensed up?"

The man got the idea and quickly began to hit the ball with better timing and rhythm.

DELAY HANDS ON DOWNSWING

The top of the backswing is the make-or-break point for rhythm and timing. If you start the down-swing with your hands ("hitting from the top"), good timing is lost.

The downswing must begin with a shifting of your weight back to the left by moving your legs, hips, and shoulders. Your hands should follow the lead of your body, your wrists remaining cocked until they release with a whiplash action as they reach the hitting area. This is what is meant by a well-timed swing.

If you have set up a proper rhythm in your back-swing, timing your downswing will be relatively easy —in fact, almost automatic.

Once the downswing starts, things begin to move fast—too fast for you to give conscious thought to the separate movements involved. But you should have an awareness that your hands are following, rather than leading, your downswing. You will, in short,

Effect of improper and proper timing on downswing. When hands improperly lead the return to the ball (left), the tension built up on the backswing (rubber band) dissipates and clubhead speed is lost. When hands remain back (right), while shoulders, hips and legs move left as downswing starts, tension (taut rubber band) is retained for later release as good clubhead speed at impact.

In a well-timed swing, clubhead speed builds up gradually on the downswing as wrists remain cocked until hands enter the hitting area.

time your downswing, so that your gradually accelerating clubhead reaches maximum speed during impact.

PRACTICE SWING IN SLOW MOTION

One excellent way to gain—or regain—good rhythm is to stand on the practice tee and hit shots in slow motion. Take, for instance, a 6-iron and hit shots of the length you would normally expect from a 9-iron. Take the club back in slow motion, and hit the shot with no more than three-quarters of your normal power. Then vary your clubs. Take a 3-iron and try to hit shots of your normal 5- or 6-iron distance. This will definitely help both your timing and your rhythm.

PRACTICE WITH A HEAVY CLUB

I mentioned in earlier chapters that by swinging an iron bar, or a golf club specially weighted with lead tape to make it three or four times heavier than normal, you can stretch and build up the muscles used in golf. This exercise is also great for improving your timing and rhythm. It will be physically impossible for you to snatch the club or bar back fast. Nor can you start your downswing with your hands. You will force yourself to swing slowly and rhythmically, and soon you will accustom your muscles to the type of swing you want to use in actual play.

12

DEVELOPING TOUCH
AROUND THE GREENS

CHIPPING

Some golfers seem to think that practicing short chips around the greens is an admission of weakness. Their idea seems to be that they will perfect their long shots and thereby eliminate the need for learning the technique of chipping up close to save a par. The majority of such golfers seems to be found among the very young. The longer a golfer plays, the more clearly he comes to understand the value of good chipping—the virtually inseparable relationship between good chipping and low scoring.

There is simply no counting the times I have seen good chipping and putting turn an apparently bad round into a good one. A player will be hitting his long shots poorly, missing fairways on tee shots and

greens on second shots—playing absolute rubbish—
and still stay right at par because of good chips and
the one-putt greens that result.

I remember playing with Doug Ford at Milwaukee
one year. He missed five of the first six greens and
still was even par. I hit all of the first six greens and
was one over par. This practical and graphic lesson
further convinced me of the need to practice chipping,
which is definitely the weakest part of my game.

Many, many times I have seen a player start out
with some bad long shots, save his pars for the first
half dozen or so holes with good chipping, and then
start hitting the ball well on all shots and score in the
60's. Without those par-saving chips on the early holes
he could never have gathered his game together for a
strong finish. Those chips built his confidence and
kept him in position to shoot a good over-all score.

There is one famous hole in particular that shows
the value of being a good chipper—the beautiful but
dangerous Number 11 at the Augusta National
Course, the scene of the Masters. There is a water
hazard that laps the edge of the green to the left.
Pull or hook the ball just a bit on the second shot and
you are in the pond.

The only sensible way to play your second shot on
this 445-yard, par-4 hole is to aim for the right edge
of the green, to leave yourself either a longish putt
or a chip from off the right fringe. More people chip
their third shots on this hole than hit the green in two.
It is very comforting on this hole to know that you are
a good chipper. This knowledge lets you play comfortably on your second shot, so you don't feel tempted
to flirt with the water at all.

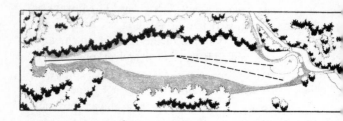

It is preferable to play the par-4, 445-yard 11th hole at the Augusta National Golf Club, scene of the annual Masters, by approaching to the right of the green, then making either a long putt or chip to the hole. A second shot hit directly at the green must skirt dangerously close to the water hazard.

Being a good chipper gives you a secure feeling anytime you are hitting a long shot to a green. You feel secure in knowing that if you miss the green you probably can make up for it with a good chip.

Before going on to some specific tips on chipping, let me list some of the best chippers I have seen during my career. My list of super-chippers would begin with Dow Finsterwald. Then there are Billy Casper, Billy Maxwell, and Doug Ford. To round out the list to five, I would include Bobby Locke. Locke was truly a fantastic chipper, even though—strangely—he used a wedge for all chips, including the ones from just off the edge of the green. This I would not advocate, despite Locke's great success with the method.

STRIKE BALL CRISPLY

The chipping techniques of all the super-chippers I have mentioned have some features all golfers could adopt. All of these men break their wrists rather quickly on their backswings, and all hit down and through the ball crisply and decisively. None uses the stiff-wristed method of chipping, which a number of pros use and advocate, and which is to me a very bad thing.

The point I want to emphasize here is that you, too, should hit these shots crisply and decisively. Don't try to "wish" the ball up there to the hole.

Plan the shot first. Decide where you want the ball to land and how much roll you want it to take. With a clear plan in mind, it is much easier to be crisp and decisive on your shot.

SELECT CLUB TO SUIT SHOT PLAN

Despite Bobby Locke's method, I definitely think that you should not do all your chipping with any one particular club. You should fit the club to the shot, depending on how much roll you want. This in turn depends on how much putting surface is between you and the hole, whether the green is fast or slow, and whether the green slopes toward you, away from you, or is level.

You should always figure on letting the ball land just a few feet beyond the edge of the putting surface nearest you. Suppose, for instance, you judged that a 5-iron chip that lands just barely on the front edge of

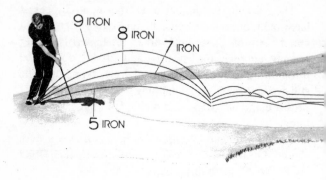

Choice of chipping club is dictated by the distance the hole is located from the front edge of the green. Always plan on landing ball a few feet onto the green, then letting it roll to cup. If target is close to front edge, use a higher-numbered iron. The further away the target, the "longer" or lower-numbered club you should use.

the green will roll just up to the cup. In that case you should take a 6-iron and let the ball land just a few feet beyond the edge of the green, a sort of safety measure. You wouldn't want to take a chance of having the ball hit short of the putting surface. It is much easier to judge the roll a ball will take after landing on the smooth, even putting surface than on the longer grass short of the green.

You look at the shot and say to yourself, "I want the ball to hit about six to ten feet beyond the front edge (a comfortable margin to give yourself) and roll the rest of the way to the cup. I think a 7-iron would

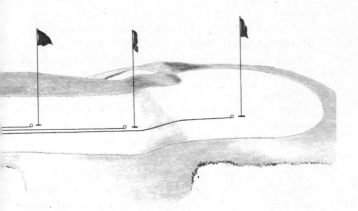

give the degree of loft and spin that would result in the amount of roll I want." So you take a 7-iron, chosen on the basis of the shot pattern you have selected.

If the ball lay just off the edge of the green and the pin was well back, you would want to take a 4-iron and turn the shot into a sort of semi-putt. With the flag on the front of the green, you would want a minimum of roll and would, of course, take the wedge. With the flag in the middle of the green, your club choice would be something between the 4-iron and the wedge.

DEVELOP "TOUCH" THROUGH PRACTICE

As in putting, touch is essential in striking the ball to finish close to the hole on a chip shot. You must develop a feel for the shot, a sense of how hard to hit the ball.

And only by practice can you develop this touch. Devote at least a third of your practice time to chipping. Practice all kinds of chips—the run-up type of shot with the irons of medium loft, the pitch and run shots with the 7-, 8-, and 9-irons, and the quick-stoppers with the wedge. Practice all the shots you are apt to want to play on the golf course.

Remember that good chipping will make you a good competitor. After you win or tie a few holes by chipping up close for one putt, the opposition will make the disheartening discovery that it is tough to win a hole from you merely by getting on the green in one shot less.

When you practice these shots, aim to have the ball land on a particular spot, just as you will be doing on the course. It is a good idea to try to pitch the ball into a bucket or something similar; this will help you a great deal in improving your touch.

DON'T BE ASHAMED TO PUTT

In connection with chipping, we must discuss here the possibility of putting from off the green. When you have a close lie on bare ground or a good lie in smooth fringe grass, the putter can be the safest and most effective club to use, even though you have to roll the ball up and over the bank of the green. Never be ashamed to putt from off the green if that is your safest shot.

Millions saw a graphic example of this shot on the last hole of the play-off in the 1966 Masters. Jack

putt from
here   putt from
                        here   chip from
                                                here

It is often best to putt a ball from off the green. This is
especially true if the ball lies on hard-packed ground (left).
If the grass is close-clipped (center), the putter may profit-
ably be used, but always chip when the grass is lush (right).

Nicklaus had missed the green to the left on his
second shot. He had two strokes over Tommy Jacobs,
who was on the front fringe of the green in two, some
30 feet from the hole.

Jack's strategy was obviously to put the ball safely
on the green with his third shot—to give himself a
putt for a par-4 and at the same time make certain
that he made no worse than a bogey-5. The ground
on which his ball lay was packed hard, having been
trampled by spectators for several days. Had he tried
to pitch the ball over the bank with a wedge, he
might easily have dumped it short or skulled (half-
topped) it over the green. He could afford to lose the
hole by one stroke, but not by two. He wisely chose
the safest course—he putted. As it happened, he
putted the ball to about 6 feet from the hole and made
his par to win by two strokes. But his strategy was
merely to insure nothing worse than a bogey.

The chipping stroke is down and through the ball. To encourage this, position hands ahead of the ball at address (left). Then hands will also be ahead of the ball at impact (center) and clubhead will bite down crisply into the ball. If hands do not lead the clubhead in the downstroke, ball will likely be topped (right).

The putt from off the green is a valuable shot to know, but don't overdo it. Don't try to roll the ball through high grass or over very bumpy ground.

LEAD WITH YOUR HANDS

On all chip shots, keep your hands in front of the clubhead so that it will come through low to the ground and strike the ball before contacting the turf. Never try to pick the ball off cleanly. Hit down and through.

Many good chippers hood the clubface a bit for this shot—they play the ball back in their stance with their hands forward. This helps produce the down-and-through chipping stroke. When you hood the clubface, you reduce the loft of the club, so make sure you choose a more lofted club than you would normally need. You might, for instance, judge that you could chip the ball onto the front edge of the green with a 6-iron and get the roll you needed. So, as a sort of safety measure, you might take a 7-iron and hood the face a bit.

"FLOAT" SHOTS FOR QUICK STOP

Frequently you will encounter a short shot that demands that you "float" the ball over a trap or bank and make it stop very quickly after it hits the green.

The wedge, your most lofted club, is the obvious choice here. The technique is to open your stance, lay back the clubface, position the ball opposite your left toe, take the club back outside the line on your back-

swing, and bring the clubhead slightly across the ball
(from outside to inside the target line) on your downswing. This gives you a nice high, soft shot that carries
a maximum amount of backspin.

The chip is a delicate shot. As in putting, there is
a tendency to get anxious and move the head too soon.
For this reason, determine to keep your head still a
bit longer than you might on a full shot. Be sure that
the ball is struck and well on its way before you turn
your head to observe the results.

13

KEYS TO SUCCESSFUL PUTTING

PUTTING

Putting is an inexact science. There are many good putters who use vastly different techniques to accomplish the same results.

The greatest putter I have ever known in my life was Bobby Locke. I would rank Arnold Palmer second. Locke used a closed stance (the right foot about 6 inches behind the left), took the putter back very definitely inside the putting line, and used rather a long backswing and a short follow-through. Palmer stands to the putt with his feet on the same line (the square stance), brings his knees in very close together, and uses a fairly short wristy stroke.

Locke was a "touch" putter; he let the ball reach the hole just as it was running out of momentum. Palmer tends to bang his putts for the back of the cup.

The next three putters on my all-time great list are

Doug Ford, Billy Casper, and Jim Ferrier, in that order. All of them differ in technique from one another and from Locke and Palmer.

Thus it is hard to lay down hard and fast rules about putting. The main things the great putters have in common is that they bring the clubhead into the ball square with the intended line; they contact the ball solidly—and they practice a lot.

If an aspiring golfer came to me with a request that I help him improve his putting, I think that I would first emphasize to him the value of good putting, hoping to inspire him to spend more time on the practice putting green.

You might think that everybody understands the value of good putting, but I rather doubt it. If they did I think that the practice putting greens of the world would be put to far greater use. I know that if I had my early life in golf to live over, I would practice putting twice as much as I did. Maybe more. Sure, everybody understands the mathematical value of a putt. If you are on the green in three and hole your first putt you make four; two-putt and you make five; three-putt and you make six, and so on.

Let's go back to that third shot, the one that put you on the green. If you had confidence in your putting ability, you probably had confidence on that shot. You knew that if you put the ball somewhere around the hole you could probably make your four. If you felt you were putting badly, you probably were thinking that unless you could lay that third shot very close to the hole you would make five or more. Such thinking would certainly have minimized the confidence you needed on that shot to the green.

When a player gets down in one putt, he puts himself in an excellent frame of mind for the tee-shot on the next hole. Good putting builds and sustains confidence all the way around the golf course. Bad putting builds fear and frustration. It is one of the marvels of the game to me that Ben Hogan can keep striking the ball so magnificently from tee to green when he knows full well that he is spotting virtually every other player in the field up to a half-dozen shots per round on the greens.

For some reason nearly all professional golfers like to disparage their own ability to putt. To hear them tell it, it's always the other fellow who makes the putts. The pros for some reason like to preserve the illusion that their good scores stem from great wood and iron shots.. More often than not this is very much an illusion.

PRACTICE A WIDE VARIETY OF PUTTS

When you practice putting, practice every type of putt—long ones, short ones, medium ones, right-breakers, left-breakers, uphill, downhill. Practice putting from the fringe of the green.

All the time you will be building up your "feel," your "touch." This touch will largely determine your success or failure on the greens. You have to depend on an unconscious inner sense to tell you how hard to strike the ball. "Inner sense" translates into touch, or feel—which comes largely from practice.

Give some extra time and attention to long putts. If you can get most of these up very close to the hole for a tap-in, you will not only lower your score, you will also save a lot of wear and tear on your nerves.

Jack Nicklaus taught me something about long putting. He takes several looks along the line between his ball and the hole. Perhaps you saw him in person or on television, when he had that long downhill putt on the 72nd hole at the 1966 Masters. He needed to make the putt to win the tournament without a play-off. He also had to two-putt to tie Tommy Jacobs and Gay Brewer and get in the play-off.

Jack studied that line half a dozen times or more. When he finally stroked that putt, its speed was perfect. It veered to the left of the cup in the last six inches. But it ran only two inches past. His study of the line really paid off.

So I advise you to take a good look at those long putts—carefully judge distance and speed.

POSITION YOUR EYES OVER THE BALL

Putting styles and techniques vary widely, even among the very best putters. But there is one point in common among virtually all good putters: they stand with their eyes directly over the ball. This is the logical position. With your eyes directly over the ball, you can look directly from the ball along the line you want the putt to take to reach the cup. You can get a true picture of the path along which the ball should travel.

Keep this tip in mind when you select a putter. Choose one with an angle between the clubhead and shaft that allows you to stand comfortably to the putt with your eyes directly over the ball, and with the sole (bottom) of the putter flush with the ground. Generally speaking, putters come in flat, medium, and

Most good putters stand with their eyes directly over the ball. During the stroke, they make absolutely certain there is no lateral body sway. The clubhead is swung back and through the ball very low to the ground.

upright "lies," the lie being the angle between club-head and shaft.

Beyond this I would not try to dictate the type of putter anybody should use. Of my five great putting experts, Locke, Palmer, and Ferrier prefer blade putters; Casper and Ford have used the mallet-head type; and I'm sure each has his preference as to putter weight.

For myself I prefer a rather heavy putter. I like to get a definite feel of the clubhead. And I like my putter to have about the same swingweight as my other clubs.

KEEP YOUR BODY STILL

Another point good putters have in common is that they keep the body still during the stroke. Bad putters tend to sway toward the hole just before the ball is struck. This may move the hands ahead of the clubhead, open the putterface, and cause the putt to be pushed to the right of the hole. It is usually anxiety that causes this forward sway. It must be resisted if you are to putt well.

The basic reason for Palmer's knock-kneed putting stance is the fact that he feels it anchors his body firmly over the ball and keeps him from moving. The same type of stance may also work for others. In any event, develop a stance in which you feel comfortable and secure over the ball, and with which you can keep your head and body still until the putt is hit and on its way.

One fine putter whose style might seem to refute this theory of keeping the body still is Kel Nagle. Kel is never still when addressing the ball. He's always moving his hands and his legs, in a sort of rhythm. Just before he starts his backswing he makes a forward press. But you can bet Kel keeps his head still while making the actual putting stroke. Otherwise he wouldn't be the great putter he is.

TAKE THE PUTTER BACK LOW

Nearly all good putters keep the clubhead low to the ground on the backswing, and I advocate doing this. I think it helps you hit the ball solidly—hit the center of the ball with the center of the clubface—and that is most important in putting. If you are going to hit the ball off-center, there is no way to judge how hard to swing the putter, and your sense of "feel" is worthless.

Billy Casper is an exception to this theory of taking the putter back low to the ground. He picks it up rather abruptly on the backswing, but he definitely makes solid contact—which you must do to putt as well as he does.

THINK POSITIVE

You must have confidence to putt well. Confidence stems basically from ability, and you can best develop ability through practice.

But you can also work mentally toward a confident attitude. When you study a putt, start with the idea that you are looking for the way to make it. Take a positive attitude.

On every putt, I draw a mental picture of the ball following the correct path directly into the center of the cup. This breeds confidence.

Don't go looking for the things that will keep the putt from going into the hole. Don't tell yourself such negative things as "I mustn't be short . . . I mustn't charge this putt too hard . . . I mustn't overplay or underplay the break."

Try to get a mental picture of the ball following the correct line and traveling at the speed needed to take it right into the middle of the cup.

I'm sure that Arnold Palmer, for instance, just doesn't allow himself to think in terms of missing a putt. All he thinks about are ways of making it.

LET CONDITIONS DETERMINE FORCE OF STROKE

Much has been made of the theory that you should putt with just enough force to make the ball die at the hole, so that it can fall in either side of the cup as well as the front. This is excellent logic if you have smooth greens.

However, the ball will more readily turn off line if it is rolling very slowly. It will take more break in the green and be more likely to bounce off line if it hits an impediment. The putt hit more firmly will hold its line better.

And then there are the old bromides like "Never up, never in" and "always get the ball to the hole." Disregard them.

Some putts call for stroking the ball firmly, as when the green is slow or the putt is sharply uphill. Under these conditions you can afford to hit the ball firmly because you won't go far beyond the cup if you miss. But on a very fast green, or when the putt is downhill, it's just not good sense to bang the putt.

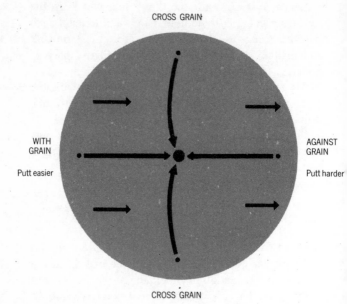

Always consider the grain of the grass as you plan your putt. In this illustration, with the grain growing from left to right, ball position could dictate one of four general ways to make the putt.

CONSIDER "GRAIN" WHEN PLANNING PUTTS

Judging the speed and undulations of the green is very important in planning putts, but many golfers fail to consider "grain," a feature of most greens. "Grain" is the direction in which the blades of grass are growing. If you are putting with the grain, the green will be slick and fast. If you are putting against the grain, the green will be slow and you will have to bang the putt firmly.

The test to determine grain simply calls for standing behind your ball and looking toward the hole. If the surface of the green looks shiny, you will be putting with the grain. If the surface presents a dull, darker appearance, you will be going against the grain. If you are putting from either side—across the grain—you can generally see the grain plainly, and you should play for the ball to turn in the direction of the grass.

Jack Nicklaus and I check the flight of one of my practice
shots. Slight alterations in the precise construction of clubs
can have a major effect on the result of any golfer's game.

14

THE RIGHT EQUIPMENT FOR YOU

The type of golf clubs you use may have more influence on your game than you suspect. Golf clubs are precision instruments. Slight changes in swing-weight, shaft flex, and grip size, especially, can result in vastly different shot results. Since golf clubs are engineered so carefully, the golfer who pays no attention to this part of his game is needlessly adding strokes to his score. Properly fitted clubs will add distance and accuracy to your shots.

Your golf professional is the person best equipped to advise you on your equipment. I can only give you some general guidelines. The professional, who can watch you swing, is the one who can get down to specifics.

Equipment is one area where the beginning golfer can immediately be on an even scale with the best tournament professional in the world, who can't get any better clubs than you can buy in your pro shop.

In general, most novice golfers tend to use clubs that are too heavy. Beginners mistakenly think that if they can just get a heavy club into motion, they'll be able to give the ball a little extra ride. That's not true. Even among today's top professionals the tendency is to use lighter clubs, for one good and simple reason— a golfer can swing a lighter club with more speed. Distance is generated more by clubhead speed than by club weight. Two plus two still equals four.

Swingweight is the major factor to consider in choosing clubs. Swingweight is the relationship of weight of the club components—grip, shaft, and head —to one another, and is measured on a special scale for that purpose. Swingweight designations range from A-0, the lightest, to E-9, the heaviest. For all practical purposes, only the C and D classifications are used.

A man beginner should probably use something near a D-0 swingweight at first; this is light enough for him to handle easily. A woman beginner will be best off in the lower C swingweights for a time. Later on, most golfers can graduate to heavier classifications. If there is a standard average, it's about C-7 for women golfers, D-3 for men.

Shaft flex, too, is of major importance. A golfer should use a shaft he can bend properly during the swing. The shaft is constantly in some state of flex as the clubhead is swung back, down, and through to the finish. Shaft flex becomes most important in the impact zone. At that time, the hands slow their forward progress and the clubhead "whips" into the ball. If a golfer is swinging clubs with the proper flex, the clubhead will move into the ball at the maximum speed the golfer can control, and the clubface will be square

Young golfers should have equipment suited to their physical capabilities. Here I show Jeff Raycroft, 10, of Augusta, Georgia, a few things about the grip.

to the target. If the shaft is too stiff, he won't get that speed, and distance. If it's too whippy, the clubface will most likely not be square to the target at impact, and accuracy will be impaired.

Shafts are designated in various ways. The most common are X—extra stiff, for the tournament professional and very long-hitting amateur; S—stiff, for the low-handicap players; R—medium stiff, used by a majority of men amateurs; A—medium, best for good women players and light-hitting men; and L—very whippy, for most women golfers.

Shaft length is surprisingly standard. The 43-inch driver can be used by a vast majority of men golfers. The reason for the small variances in this area is that most people's hands are about the same distance from the ground when the arms are hanging straight down. Tall persons usually have longer arms, and shorter persons shorter arms.

The type of swing you have is more of a determining factor of shaft length than is your height. If you have a flat swing, you will need longer clubs to reach the ball. If your swing is very upright, you could use shorter shafts, since you play the ball closer to your feet. Here is another place your professional can be of great assistance.

Whatever shaft you use, the clubhead should lie flat on the ground at address. If the toe is off the ground, your clubhead lie is too upright. If you hook consistently, this could be your trouble, for a too-upright club lie will cause shots to curve from right to left. The opposite is true if the heel is off the ground. Then your lie is too flat, and you may be plagued with slices to the right.

Grips are a matter of personal preference, with

only a few rules to bear in mind. People with large hands or long fingers need a bigger grip than the one for those with small hands or short fingers.

I use the G-grip, which is tapered to a smaller dimension at the top than at the bottom. The fingers that grip the club at the top end are smaller; a smaller grip size automatically makes them more secure. Many other golfers use standard grips, which are tapered in the other direction, and do quite well.

I prefer leather in the grip because it gives me a firmer feeling than composition material does. Again, this is a matter of personal preference. The type of grip that feels good for you will be best for you.

A beginning golfer should definitely *not* use a high-compression golf ball. He simply cannot swing hard enough to compress it at impact; he'll feel he is hitting a rock. Novice players should use a lower-compression ball, around 85. As he improves his game, he can graduate to better balls.

And here's one tip anyone can use. In cold weather, a lower-compression ball will fly farther than those more tightly wound. Of course, when it's hot, the high-compression balls are the ones to hit. Change golf balls, within reason, under these conditions.

I might add that the golfer who wants to play his best should also consider his clothing, including shoes. Golf clothing should be as light as the weather permits—and neat. I've always felt that the golfer who dresses well gives himself a plus, for he'll feel better and probably play superior golf as a consequence

15

GOLF IS MY LIFE

Golf has been my life. It has brought me many financial rewards since I chose to make the game my profession. It has enabled me to travel all over the world and to make so many good friends I couldn't possibly count them.

Nevertheless, even if I had not taken up golf for a living, I would have enjoyed playing the game on a casual basis. No other sport offers golf's peculiar challenge. It will build the character of anyone who takes it seriously enough to do his best. Grousing when things are going the wrong way does absolutely no good. Crowing when you're on top marks you as a person most people wouldn't like to know in any walk of life.

When you're in the midst of a round, no one can help you. You must do your own thinking, make your own shots. There are no crutches. There are no teammates to bail you out. In the end, golf brings out your best—or worst. In an overwhelming majority of cases, the best prevails.

Another thing I particularly like about golf is the fact that it can be enjoyed and played by people of all ages. Children enjoy its challenge, and it helps them develop strong character. Seniors can go on getting exercise in this gentle but entertaining manner for many years. With something like golf to concentrate on, older persons maintain a healthier outlook on life. They don't have either time or inclination to worry about growing old; they're having too much fun.

There isn't much use in playing golf haphazardly, however. For a person to maintain keen interest, he must play a game that is at least decent in his own eyes. If there is no prospect for eventual improvement, he might as well junk it all and take up some less demanding avocation.

Pay attention to your conditioning, one well-marked avenue to good golf. This includes both a proper exercise routine and a sensible diet. No one can apply himself if he's out of shape.

Keep your mind in constant action as you play. Think of swing points that have helped you in the past. Play the percentages so far as course strategy is concerned. Don't take unnecessary chances, but don't be so weak-kneed as not to go after the "impossible" shot on occasion. That's much of the fun of golf—bringing off a great shot, especially when your opponent may have thought you boxed in.

When you wish to polish a certain part of your game, go to the practice tee and work on it. Try different things. When one works, try it again—and again and again—until it becomes firmly embedded in your swing. You can nail down fundamentals on the practice tee. Start with your grip and stance. No one can play well without good fundamentals.

I've always thought that the most important basic of the backswing is the full shoulder turn, with your left shoulder turning to a point directly under your chin at the top of your backswing.

On the downswing, see that your weight returns to your left foot at once. Pull the club down with your left hand; keep your left arm straight and your head steady, and finish with your hands high. That's an extreme but nevertheless sound simplification of the swing.

Don't expect everything to work out all the time, no matter how hard you apply yourself. Although I've been lucky and have had relatively few disappointments in golf, there have been some heartbreaks.

In the 1962 Masters at the Augusta National Golf Club, I tied with Arnold Palmer and Dow Finsterwald with 280 after 72 holes. Dow and I played steadily in the fourth round, but Arnie's 18 was up and down. I was paired with him and he made a couple of shots that were fantastic. On the par-3 16th, for instance, he chipped in a 40-foot downhill shot for a two. On the par-4 17th, he knocked his approach through the trees to the green and birdied again.

It was the play-off that hurt me. After nine, I was three shots ahead of Palmer. Finsterwald was not in contention by then. On the 10th, I hit my 5-iron approach right at the flag, but the ball hit a rough spot and rolled off the back edge. My chip stopped 5 feet from the cup. When I missed that putt—the ball "looked in" but stayed on the lip—I had lost two shots of my lead, for Palmer birdied the hole. He went on to win the play-off with a remarkable 31 on the back nine. My play on that particular hole, especially that five-footer I missed, was the most disappointing experience of my golfing life. I can sympathize with Arnie and his collapse on the back nine in the fourth round of the 1966 U.S. Open. But disappointments are part of golf, and you must be strong-minded enough to bounce back.

Thrills I've had plenty, but none more exciting than when I won the 1965 U.S. Open at the Bellerive Country Club near St. Louis. That victory completed the major golf ambition of my life. Even before I began to play golf on an international scale, I set a goal of winning the four major championships—the British Open, the U.S. Open, the PGA Championship, and the Masters. Only Gene Sarazen and Ben Hogan had been able to do this before, and when Jack Nicklaus won the 1966 British Open, he made it too.

In 1958, at twenty-two, I played in my first British Open. I remember watching Peter Thomson and David Thomas putting on the last green; I was not in contention. If either could make his putt, he would be the winner, and if Thomas did it, he'd be the youngest, at twenty-four, ever to win the title. Well, both missed, and Thomson won the play-off, so I still had a chance to be the youngest winner. But my victory would have to come in 1959, when I was twenty-three.

That year I went to Muirfield, in Scotland, ten days before the championship. Wind makes a great deal of difference in how a course should be played, and, knowing it often blew there, I wanted to get in plenty of practice. The wind, however, blew in the *opposite* direction all during the practice rounds, not in the prevailing direction. Nevertheless, I tried to keep in mind distances and clubs which would be pertinent should things get back to normal when play started.

Despite all of my practice, I found myself eight shots behind Flory van Donck of Belgium and Fred Bullock of Great Britain going into the final day's play, which then consisted of thirty-six holes. I was hitting the ball well, however, and still felt I could win, especially since van Donck had been quoted as saying I couldn't because my swing was too flat. Such statements will make anyone all the more determined to do well.

The wind did turn around to normal on that last day, and my practice paid off. I knew how to handle it. I came to the 72nd hole needing a par-4 for a 66. On this very narrow hole, I drove into a trap on the left, 6-ironed to the front edge, and then chipped onto the green. When I 3-putted for a 6, I thought I had blown my chances, for Bullock and van Donck were still on the course and definitely in contention.

I had time to go to the hotel and shower, then watch from a balcony as they finished. They were unsuccessful, and I had won the British Open with a 284, at twenty-three the youngest ever to do so. Thus I completed my first step toward taking the four big ones.

Whenever I drive down the pine-lined entrance road of the Augusta National Golf Club in Augusta, Ga. I almost choke up. This site of the Masters is one of the most inspiring in golf. And I know that Ernest Nipper, my regular caddie there and one of the best I've ever known, will be waiting with words of encouragement.

In 1961, I went to Augusta just three days before

the Masters. My concentration was at a peak. People
tell me I seemed almost in a state of self-hypnosis.
During the third round, I was at one time four strokes
ahead of Arnold Palmer, my closest rival and the de-
fending champion. While I was on the 11th green,
one of the heaviest rains I've ever seen fell, and the
round was washed out. I was disappointed, of course,
to have my probable lead canceled.

I did manage to stay ahead in the third round, but
disaster struck in the fourth. I took a 7 on the par-5
13th and a 6 on the par-5 15th. Three over par in two
holes. I could only par in, and sat in the clubhouse
with my 280, leading the field. But Palmer was to
come. All he eventually needed was a par-4 on the
18th to win.

Arnie hit his approach into the right-hand trap,
and I was amazed at the way he played the sand shot.
His ball was partially buried, but he left the face of his
sand wedge wide open. Mr. Bob Jones, who was with
me, noticed this also, and said Arnie was playing the
shot incorrectly. "He should close the face and pop it
out," Mr. Jones remarked. Sure enough, Palmer
skulled the ball across the green, finally taking a 6 for
a 281. I had won the second of the four titles, the first
foreign-born player to take the Masters.

Of all the world's great tournaments, I believe the
PGA Championship has the strongest field. Add to
this my mental and physical state when the 1962
Championship was played, and it didn't seem I had
much of a chance. I had just played very badly in the
British Open at Troon, failing to make the 36-hole
cut. When I arrived at Philadelphia's Aronimink
course for the PGA, I was exhausted. I told my man-

ager, Mark McCormack, that I wouldn't be surprised if I failed to make the cut there, too.

But when I started practicing, I fell in love with Aronimink. Trees were everywhere, adding to the course's beauty and challenge. Fairway bunkers were strategically positioned. (Incidentally, I believe you'll play better if you find something you like about a course, rather than something that you don't like. This will work for anyone, playing anywhere. Make friends with the course.)

In four days, I did a complete turnaround. By the time the tournament started, I was full of confidence. I'll never forget that first drive. The 1st hole has an elevated tee with an out-of-bounds on the left and long rough on the right. I took out a 4-wood, aimed to the right and drew the ball back onto the fairway. I used my 4-wood off the tee almost exclusively all through the tournament.

In the fourth round, I was involved in a battle with Bob Goalby, my playing partner of the day. Bob had started play four shots back, but he was charging. He drew within one shot when he birdied the 541-yard 16th, almost holing out for an eagle from a sand trap.

On the last hole, I drove into some trees on the right, 6- or 7-iron distance from the green, but the trees blocked my path. I had a good lie, however. For my approach, I used a 3-iron, setting myself up for a slice and fading the ball sweet and low around those trees and onto the green. I 2-putted for my par, and won with 278 to Goalby's 279. (Should you ever be in a situation similar to mine after my drive on 18, remember that it is much easier to slice (or hook) a longer club than a short iron. Position yourself for

Jack Nicklaus and I came to the Bellerive Country Club near St. Louis, Missouri, a week early to practice for the 1965 U.S. Open.

the type of shot you want, but don't swing quite as hard as usual.)

I had always thought I would win the biggest of them all, the U.S. Open, before the other major championships. I had felt this because most courses over which this tournament is played always emphasize accuracy, not distance. And hitting straight shots, I felt, was one of my strong points.

By the time the 1965 U.S. Open rolled around, I had gone without a major title for three years. I was determined to make a good showing at the Bellerive Country Club. To this end, I made a careful "map"

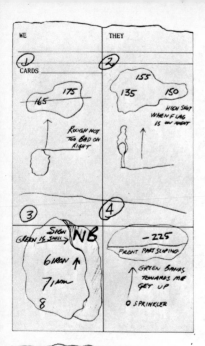

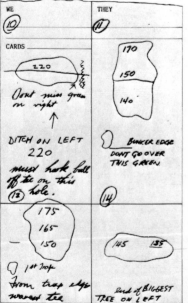

These are the diagrams and notes I made during practice rounds at Bellerive before the 1965 U.S. Open. Every hole was considered except 13 and 16, both par-3's. The numbers of the holes are circled. The numbers on the greens indicate various dis-

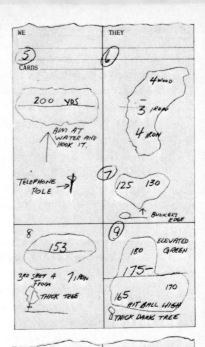

tances from the object in the fairway, such as a sand trap, a tree, or a water sprinkler near which I expected my drives to finish. Armed with this information, I knew exactly what club I should use for every approach.

of Bellerive, jotting down in a notebook distances to the greens from certain points, along with a drawing of the holes and the exact shape and contour of the greens. My notebook turned out to be invaluable, for no matter where I was on the fairway, I knew exactly what club to use for my next shot. I was also familiar with how the ball rolled from various points on the greens.

On every hole I visualized how I would play it—from the tee shot to the final putt. I was determined to have the patience to play this course the *right* way.

Bellerive is one of the most difficult courses I've ever played, so good planning was a must. Bunkers, trees, water, rough—every imaginable hazard was there. At 7,191 yards, it was also the longest course in Open history.

In the fourth round, I reached the 10th hole three shots ahead of Kel Nagle, my nearest competitor. I was playing directly behind Kel, and saw almost every one of his shots. I saw him birdie 10, and when I bogeyed I was only one shot ahead! Nagle also birdied 12, from 30 feet, but I matched that with my own birdie from 15 feet.

While the lead bounced back and forth after that, Nagle and I eventually tied with 282, and the next day I won the play-off 71 to 74. That completed my Grand Slam of Golf.

Winning these four tournaments, plus becoming the first foreign golfer to be the leading money-winner on the U.S. tournament circuit (in 1961) and posting the lowest American scoring average for a year (also in 1961) rang down the curtain on my major golfing goals. This doesn't mean that I won't keep playing and

.ng to win anything I enter, but I won't be com-
ting so often in the future.

Actually, I want to delve more deeply into youth
work in my native South Africa, and continue an
even closer association with my farming interests
there. I would like to leave tournament golf when I'm
forty, but before I quit I hope to fulfill my very last
golf goal—to break 60 in an international event on a
championship course.

More Corgi Titles for Sports Enthu

GRAND SLAM GOLF   Gary

7/6d   55:

The astonishing success story of the 'little man' of g
from modest beginnings back home in South Africa, succ
by a total dedication to the physical and mental demands o
game in reaching the very heights of professional golf.
"All splendid stuff that no golfer at any level should miss.
Sunday Telegraph

POWER GOLF   Ben Hogan

5/-   552 00589 4

Another angle on golf . . . HOW *YOU* CAN SUCCEED . . . . Ben
Hogan's detailed description of his grip, his stance and his swing.
Advice on how to develop your powers of concentration, how
to practise and eight simple hints on how to lower your score.
A book you daren't be without!

JOGGING   William J. Bowerman and W. E. Harris M.D.

5/-   552 07995 2

A medically approved programme that will REDUCE THE WAIST-
LINE, IMPROVE YOUR APPEARANCE, HELP PROLONG YOUR
LIFE. Jogging is a simple type of exercise, requiring no highly
developed skills. Its great appeal is that it is so handy—anyone
can do it anywhere. It's free, it's safe and it's fun.

All these great books are available at your local bookshop or newsagent; or can be ordered direct from the publisher. Just tick the titles you want and fill in the form below.

CORGI BOOKS, Cash Sales Department, J. Barnicoat (Falmouth) Ltd., P.O. Box 11, Falmouth, Cornwall.

Please send cheque or postal order. No currency, PLEASE. Allow 6d. per book to cover the cost of postage and packing in U.K., 9d. per copy overseas.

NAME ....

ADDRESS ....

(May 69) ....